Longman Keys to Language Teaching

Series Editor: Neville Grant

Essentials of English Language Teaching

Julian Edge

Longman

London • New York

Longman Group UK Limited,
Longman House, Burnt Mill, Harlow,
Essex CM20 2JE, England
and Associated Companies throughout the world.

Distributed in the United States of America
by Longman Publishing, New York

First published 1993

British Library Cataloguing in Publication Data
Edge, Julian
     Essentials of English Language Teaching –
     (Longman Keys to Language Teaching Series)
     I. Title II. Series
     428.2071
     ISBN 0–582–02565–6

Library of Congress Cataloguing in Publication Data
Edge, Julian, 1948 –
        The essentials of English language teaching/Julian Edge.
           p.   cm. — (Longman keys to language teaching)
        Includes bibliographical references.
        ISBN 0–582–02565–6
        1. English language — Study and teaching —
        Foreign speakers.
        2. English language — Study and teaching.
        I. Title.   II. Series.
        PE1128.A2E275   1993
        428'.007 — dc20

Set in   9½/11½ pt Century Schoolbook

Produced by Longman Singapore Publishers Pte Ltd.
Printed in Singapore

ISBN 0-582-02565-6

Acknowledgements
We are grateful to the following for permission to
reproduce copyright material:

Cambridge University Press for an extract from *The
New Cambridge English Course 1* by Michael Swan
and Catherine Walter (1990). © Michael Swan and
Catherine Walter 1990; Zomba Music Publishers Ltd
for an extract from the song 'The Price You Pay'
words and music by Bruce Springsteen.
© 1980 Bruce Springsteen (ASCAP).

We are grateful to the following for permission to
reproduce copyright illustrative material:

Cambridge University Press for pages 23 (top right),
35, 45 (top), 62, 93, 117 and 119; Jet for page 102;
Longman Group (UK) Ltd for page 23 (bottom left),
31, 41, 45 (bottom), 67, 72, 86, 100 and 110; Penguin
Books Ltd for page 94.

Contents

4

Preface

In 1992, I participated in Bulgaria's first IATEFL conference in Sophia. After one of my talks, a young American approached me and told me he had just started teaching English in Bulgaria. He had asked his university ESL Department to recommend a 'survivor's guide'. They suggested he should take a copy of *Making the most of your Textbook* – one of the first books in the *Keys* series. Next time I hope they will suggest this book by Julian Edge, too!

For some time, it has been clear to us that a demand has arisen for a general book in the *Keys* style: a book which can serve as a first introduction for those new to the field, and which can also give experienced teachers a fresh perspective on what is happening in ELT today. So, this is our latest title: *Essentials of English Language Teaching*.

True to the *Keys* style, it is straightforward in its expression and practical in its suggestions, while avoiding over-simplistic lists of things to do. It expresses our belief that teachers who understand what is going on in their classrooms will make the best decisions about what to do next.

In a paradoxical way this book both demystifies English Language Teaching, and at the same time indicates that it is a more complex activity than is sometimes thought. It does not bang the usual, now rather clichéd drum that ELT can be broadly reduced to 'PPP' – Presentation, Practice and Production. It shows rather that these three stages are in fact oversimplifications – and that they are not really self-contained stages at all.

Our field is expanding all the time. More and more teachers are taking introductory ELT Certificate courses of one kind or another in Britain, in the United States and all over the world. And a lot more are jumping in at the deep end! Anyone who has read this book will be ready to make a start in ELT. I wish I had had a book like it when I started!

Neville Grant

You make up your mind, you choose the chance you take.

Bruce Springsteen

To Karolina, who will do things differently

Acknowledgements

The opening lines of Chapter 7 come from working with Pat Grounds in one of my best teaching experiences. Apart from that and the work acknowledged in the references, the debts and the sources have become too entangled to acknowledge separately. My sincere thanks to all the students and colleagues I have worked with. As far as the writing is concerned, special thanks to Damien Tunnacliffe for commissioning the book in the first place and for his continuing interest and support; also to Neville Grant, Alyson Lee and Lisa Howard for comments on the manuscript and their tireless work in the production of the book.

Introduction

Who is this book for?

It's for people approaching English Language Teaching for the first time who want a clear description of the field and advice on how to get started. It's also for experienced teachers who would like an opportunity to reflect on their own work.

What exactly do we mean by 'English Language Teaching'?

What British writers usually call *Teaching English as a Foreign Language (TEFL)* and *Teaching English as a Second Language (TESL)*, and what American writers usually call *Teaching English to Speakers of Other Languages (TESOL)*. The abbreviation *ELT* is used throughout the book.

Does the book explain the best way of teaching English?

It gives examples of teaching methods and materials and relates these to basic principles. It makes suggestions and gives advice. Each teacher then has to make appropriate decisions for his or her own classroom. There is no single 'best way'; there are teachers who use their intelligence, knowledge, experience, skills, sensitivity, creativity and awareness to help other people learn.

Is this a practical book?

Definitely: it gives clear guidelines about how to teach English in class, using lots of examples of modern materials. Remember also that a practical teacher is a thinking person who has to keep making decisions about what to do. Readers can make the book even more practical by doing the activities which review each chapter.

Does the book tell me all I need to know?

No, but it provides the essentials to help you make a good start, and recommends titles for further reading. In addition, the last chapter suggests ways in which you can support your own continuing development, and for anyone studying for a teaching qualification, there is advice on classroom assessment and writing.

Part One
Familiarisation

In this part of the book, we shall look into ELT classrooms in order to familiarise ourselves with what we find there. We will encounter the main elements of ELT in any situation:

- the people;
- the processes of language learning and teaching;
- aspects of the language itself;
- the language learning materials that are usually available;
- the classroom environment and kinds of equipment that you might use.

At the same time, we shall see how these elements are involved in practical teaching techniques.

While you work on the ideas in the book, think about the actual details of your own situation, or of situations you have known as a language learner or teacher. Do the ideas in the book match up with your experience? Can you be specific?

The activities at the end of each chapter also summarise the chapter. They are meant to help you enrich your reading with your experience and enrich your experience with your reading. They will be of most use if you have a friend or colleague to discuss them with. In that way, you can develop your ideas as you talk and listen.

People

If you look into a classroom in use, the first thing you expect to see is people. In this chapter, we shall look at the people most obviously involved in English Language Teaching: learners and teachers.

Learners

All learners are the same. Outside class, they have a family, friends, work, study or play, responsibilities, a place to live, and all the joys and sorrows that come with those things. Into class, they bring with them their names, their knowledge, experience, intelligence, skills, emotions, imagination, awareness, creativity, sense of humour, problems, purposes, dreams, hopes, aspirations, fears, memories, interests, blind spots, prejudices, habits, expectations, likes, dislikes, preferences, and everything else that goes with being a human being, including the ability to speak at least one language.

All learners are different. No two individuals have the same knowledge, or skills, or expectations, or any of the other things listed in the last paragraph. Learners are also influenced by their age and by their educational, social and cultural backgrounds, which they may or may not share with their fellow students and teacher.

Some learners are more successful than others. These characteristics are typical of good language learners, although no learner would have them all:

1 They have a positive attitude about the language they want to learn and about speakers of that language.

2 They have a strong personal motivation to learn the language.

3 They are confident that they will be successful learners.

4 They are prepared to risk making mistakes and they learn from the mistakes that they make.

5 They like to learn about the language.

6 They organise their own practice of the language.

7 They find ways to say things that they do not know how to express correctly.

8 They get into situations where the language is being used and they use the language as often as they can.

9 They work directly in the language rather than translate from their first language.

10 They think about their strategies for learning and remembering and they consciously try out new strategies.

What do we learn from all this as teachers?

Firstly, we must not see the learners in front of us as language learning machines; they may have many other things on their minds. Nor is language learning just an intellectual process. All the aspects of humanity listed in the first paragraph about learners have to be expressed through language and can all be used to enrich language learning. To learn a language is to learn to express your*self*.

Secondly, we have to make an effort to inform ourselves about our learners. If we share a cultural and linguistic background with them, this is to our advantage. All teachers have to be sensitive to social distinctions and they have to try to be open to the personal needs, learning purposes and learning styles of individuals.

Thirdly, we have to make our classrooms places where the characteristics of good learners are encouraged. We then have to help individuals discover which positive characteristics suit their own personality, society and culture. Some, for instance, will learn better through lots of exposure to natural language, while some will learn better through study and practice. Make sure that your students understand this.

> We try to teach all our students, but the successful ones are usually those who take on some responsibility for their own learning.

Teachers

Teacher success can be measured most obviously by how much their students learn. Like learners, however, all teachers are different, and it is a good idea to recognise straight away that you are unlikely simply to be 'a good teacher'. You can be a great teacher for some people, an alright teacher for some, and you will be a poor teacher for others.

> The challenge is to go on developing into the teacher you most want to be.

The teacher is the most powerful person in the classroom. There are many ways for the teacher to use that power. These are the most important things that need to be taken care of:

- *Organisation* – Learners must feel that their activity is purposeful, that they are putting their efforts into a framework they can trust. Learners need just enough structure so that they feel supported, and just enough freedom so that they have room for themselves to grow.
- *Security* – If learners feel safe, they will be more able to take part in the lesson. If they feel that everyone in class, including the teacher, is on the same side, they may risk making mistakes that they can learn from.
- *Motivation* – Some learners will be motivated to learn for external reasons, which is a big help, but all learners need to be involved in classwork. This happens best when they are motivated by interesting tasks, when they experience success, and when they see the relevance of classwork to their outside lives.
- *Instruction* – Learners need to be told new things, and told how to do new things.
- *Modelling* – Learners need to be shown new things, and shown how to do new things.
- *Guidance* – Learners need a helping hand to discover new things and to practise new skills.
- *Information* – Learners need sources of extra information about what they are learning, which they can call on as required.
- *Feedback* – Learners need to know how close they are getting to their targets. Was that meaning clear? Was the verb correct?
- *Encouragement* – Learners need to feel that the language is developing inside them, even if what they are producing at the moment seems unlike standard English.

● *Evaluation* – Some learners have external standards that must be reached, important examinations to pass or fail. They need to know where they stand.

So, can we say that the teacher must organise, provide security, motivate, instruct, model, guide, inform, give feedback, encourage and evaluate? Yes, but the best teachers do something else, too. In a way that suits the individuals, society and culture concerned, they encourage learners to take on some responsibility in these areas.

> We aim to help learners become independent of teachers, so that learners can use what they learn and continue to learn on their own.

There is one unfortunate characteristic of teaching which we must mention now. Teachers work alone. One of the most terrifying words in teaching is *observation*: it means having someone else in your classroom who is not one of the students. Observation has always been connected with being assessed, and this introduces tension and fear. Because of this fear, teachers do not share experiences with colleagues and seldom really learn from each other.

> The single most important change we can hope for in teaching is for teachers who trust each other to visit each other's lessons, not to evaluate, but to share.

The sooner you start, the easier it is, and the more you will learn. We return to this topic in Chapter 11.

Teachers, of course, have as many differences between them as do learners and cooperation has to be based on respect for our differences. Let's finish this chapter by investigating one important area of difference.

Read the statements below based on Briggs-Myers (1980). If you had to choose, which one do you think comes closer to describing you? Are you basically an S sort of a person, or an N sort of a person?

S	N
I am good at learning how things really are from practical experience.	I am good at seeing possibilities which might not be obvious.
I enjoy using my eyes, ears and other senses to find out what is happening.	I enjoy using my imagination to work on how things could be.

S	N
I get great satisfaction from using my skills to do what I do well.	I get great satisfaction from learning new skills.
I don't enjoy facing one new problem after the other.	I don't enjoy facing the same problem repeatedly.
I am patient over details, but I don't like situations to get too complicated.	I don't mind complicated situations, but I get impatient over details.

None of us is purely one type or the other, but a lot of people do feel closer to one of these descriptions than the other. This distinction can be very important in our work and cooperation. If you can make a choice, please do so before you read on.

People who choose S tend to live through their senses and have a good grasp of the way things are. People who choose N tend to live through their intuitions and have a good grasp of possibilities. Neither of these types is better than the other, but we can expect them to have different attitudes towards new ideas. Two people can hear the same teaching suggestion, and while one says:
No, that won't work here.   (= *That's not the way things are.*)
the other one says:
Yes, we could do that.   (= *That should be possible.*)

Unfortunately, this often begins as a disagreement and ends with a judgement of the other person. So, one says, 'He's hopelessly impractical!' and the other one says, 'She's got no imagination at all!' What we need to do is to recognise each other's strengths.

If you find that people often respond to your ideas by saying that they are impractical, take some time to consider the fact that some people might have a much better sense than you do of the way things actually are. If you find that you yourself often reject people's ideas as impractical, take some time to consider that some people might have a much better sense than you do of the way that things could be. You may still want to disagree, but remember two things:

> The difference between 'a practical suggestion' and 'just a theoretical idea' might lie in you.

> A useful technique for you might not be so useful for someone else, and vice-versa.

> *In this chapter, we have emphasised the importance of thinking about learners and teachers as whole people whose individuality can be a source of learning. The questions and activities which follow are designed to help you review and reflect on the chapter in personal terms.*

Questions and activities

Think about your responses and then discuss them with a colleague.

1 What do you think about the idea of bringing the learners' outside life into class? Have you any ideas or experience of how this can be done?

2 Look at the characteristics of good language learners on pages 9–10. Do you recognise them? Are they true of you? Are they true of good language learners you have known? Can you think of other characteristics of good language learners?

3 Who were the best teachers you have had? What was so good about them? Did it have anything to do with their way of treating you as a person? Can you relate their teaching to the list of things on pages 11–12 that have to be taken care of in class?

4 Look at that list again. One way to help students move towards independence is for the teacher to share the responsibility for these areas with learners. Would that be possible in your situation? How?

5 Find someone you can trust and ask him or her to watch you teach. Afterwards, tell your observer about two things that went well. Your observer does not need to tell you anything. You will be surprised how much you can learn.

6 What did you think about the S and N difference? Is this of any practical use to a teacher, or just of possible theoretical interest?

 # Learning and teaching processes

The people that we see in the ELT classroom are involved in processes which we want to understand. In this chapter, we look at two basic ways in which people learn foreign languages. We then examine the responses which ELT has developed to support language learning. These ideas underlie the methodological suggestions which follow throughout the book.

Language learning

The key to learning is motivation. Never forget that.

There are two ways in which people learn a foreign language:

- *Consciously*, through formal learning. In this situation, learners study the language in the sequence in which it is presented to them, usually following an organised syllabus. This kind of learning tends to encourage accuracy in the language, as well as knowledge of what is correct. Learners develop their fluency and feeling for what is socially appropriate in the language outside this learning, according to the actual demands made on them to communicate.
- *Subconsciously*, by 'picking it up'. This is typically the case when learners are in a situation where they are exposed to lots of natural language use. This kind of learning tends to encourage fluency in the language, as well as a natural feel for what is socially appropriate. In this kind of natural learning, different learners seem to acquire the grammar of the language in more or less the same sequence: the language develops along its own path inside the learner. The level of formal accuracy achieved depends on the demands made on the learner to become more accurate.

These two ways of learning can also support each other. For instance, when I naturally acquire a new way of saying something in German,

I later analyse how that piece of language works grammatically. On the other hand, when I am studying one area of German, I may pick up some other bit of language without being aware of it at the time.

Language teaching

In terms of broad approach, there are two ways to teach people to use a language:

1 Move step by step from form to meaning, adding together different bits of the language which have been isolated for learning. Item by item, you:
   - Provide a model.
   - Get the students to copy the model.
   - Get the students to personalise the model by using it to express something they want to say.

2 Move from meaning to form. That is:
   - Put the students in a situation where they want to communicate something.
   - Encourage them to communicate as best they can.
   - Focus the students' attention on the forms used to achieve communication (if you find that this is necessary).

As people, we might develop a preference for one approach over the other. As teachers, we will make sure that we use both approaches, and mix them together, in order to be fair to the preferences of different learners. Some learners will dislike copying models, as some will dislike being called upon to communicate before they have been taught all the necessary forms. Some will be confused by any focus on forms without meaningful use.

> Learners who are aware of their own preferences and the preferences of others can better appreciate what is happening in class and better support their own learning outside class.

By focusing sometimes on form and sometimes on meaning, we try to get students to take advantage of both subconscious and conscious learning. In addition, we encourage them to think about their learning and become better learners.

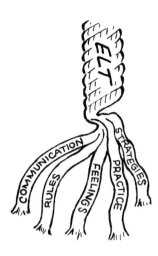

So, we have three mental levels to work at:

- subconscious learning
- conscious learning
- awareness of learning.

We are now going to look at five basic strands of ELT which are usually all woven together. They arise from different views of language learning, which is why it is easy to pick them apart. But our interest is not to follow these ideas back to where they came from, it is to see how they all give strength to the current ELT scene. They are: *communication, feelings, rules, practice,* and *strategies*.

At the end of the chapter, there are some ELT materials which exemplify the different strands.

Communication

Communication is at the heart of modern ELT, and this section of the chapter relates to all the others which follow. Let us look at two reasons why communication is so important.

Communication is the goal of language teaching

People usually learn English because for some reason, in some way, they want to be able to communicate in English. When this is not the case, as with schoolchildren or students following compulsory courses, we still look for some kind of communicative goal as a way of motivating them. Some examples would be:

- being able to sing the words of your favourite pop songs;
- reading what an English newspaper wrote about your national soccer team;
- listening to a foreigner talk about life in your city;
- investigating a problem from your academic discipline.

Communication is part of the learning process

- As we communicate, we make our formally learnt language more automatically available. If, for example, I have just learnt how to ask questions with the verb *to have*, I can ask my classmates if they have any brothers or sisters and 'Do you have . . .' becomes part of my English.
- During meaningful communication, we acquire language subconsciously. To continue the same example, while I am practising *Do you have* . . . in 'Do you have any brothers and

sisters?', I may acquire this correct use of *any* and develop a feel for its use without explicit teaching.

- When we are making an effort to communicate, we develop strategies of communication which help us learn. At its simplest, I remember needing the German word for *snail* in the middle of a conversation. I used words that I did know to make up 'worm-with-house'. Everyone laughed and I learnt the word *Schnecke*.

So, what do we know about communication? We know that it involves more than language, but here we are going to concentrate on linguistic communication. We can say that:

- We communicate in order to get, give, or exchange information, e.g:
  What's the capital of Ecuador?

- We communicate in order to do things and get things done, e.g:
  Please wake me at 6.30.

- The way we communicate with someone expresses and develops our relationship with that person. Compare:
  I want this ready by 5.30.
  with
  Do you think you might be able to have this ready by 5.30?

- People from different societies and cultures mean and do different things by what they say. They have different ideas about politeness.

- You can never be absolutely sure what someone is going to say.

So, as a foreign language learner, I need to know how to:

- get my message across;
- get things done;
- be polite;
- avoid judging other people according to my own values;
- deal with the unexpected.

These issues are especially important in ELT, because so many people are motivated to learn English as the language of international communication. We must not, however, think that these issues can be separated from the grammar, pronunciation and other parts of the language system itself. In the above example, the relationship is directly connected to the use of the modal form *might*. And if students are learning English in order to pass exams or write reports, for instance, they will need to write accurately and coherently if they are going to succeed. Simply 'getting a message across' will probably not satisfy their examiners or their bosses.

So, English language teachers have to balance the teaching of the English language system with the teaching of an ability to communicate in English.

Or we might describe the students' task as juggling with three clubs, as they learn to communicate and meet the demands of:

● *accuracy*   – conforming to the language system itself;
● *fluency*   – operating the system quickly and easily;
● *appropriacy* – relating successfully to other people through the language.

Ideas about communication are at the centre of modern ELT, as we shall see repeatedly throughout the rest of this book. The communicative strand of ELT relates to conscious and subconscious learning, and to accuracy as well as to fluency and appropriacy.

Feelings

We have already mentioned the importance of the learner's motivation, attitude, confidence, security, and willingness to take risks. There is another reason why we put so much emphasis on the importance of a positive emotional environment in the language class. The secure, motivated learner is prepared to make a personal investment in learning. That is, learners will talk about themselves and about things that matter to them. In this atmosphere, they will also listen with respect to what others have to say. The foreign language then starts to perform the normal functions of language: people are saying things they care about and are establishing relationships with other people. When language use is as meaningful as this, it is also memorable: language learning takes place.

Positive emotional involvement leads to effective learning.

There are some dangers here. We do not want to pry into people's lives, or in any way oblige people to talk about topics which might be painful for them. Two points to remember are:

● Activities which deal with positive emotions are preferred.
● Students must always have some way out of activities which they consider too personal.

As long as we remember these notes of caution, we will find modern ELT provides many useful activities (often called *humanistic*) which call on learners to share personal information through English. Such activities can be effective when used by a sensitive teacher, but they are not magic formulas for making teachers sensitive. When used insensitively, they are powerfully demotivating.

This strand of ELT is connected with subconscious learning and with fluency and appropriacy. It is also connected with the idea that learners must be involved as whole human beings in their language learning.

Rules

The rules we are talking about here are rules which attempt to describe the way English actually is, not rules which tell people what they ought to say. So we are talking about *descriptive* rules such as: The third person singular of the Present Simple ends with the sound /s/ , /z/ or /ɪz/, e.g: *This puppet walks, sings and dances.*

We do not mean *prescriptive* rules of the kind: You should not end a sentence with a preposition.

Rules of language are important for one very good reason:

> A rule is a small thing to learn, but it can have big results.

For example, once you have learnt that English makes a past tense by adding *-ed* to a verb, you can make a past tense of any verb you want to, and you will almost certainly be understood. As you continue to learn, you can make better rules, especially if you pay attention to how the language works, and learn from your mistakes.

It is not enough simply to tell students rules. To make students more active, we can give them a rule and ask them to use it in producing some language. Or, we give students examples of new language and then show them what the rule is. Or, we give examples and ask students to work out what the rule is.

This strand of ELT is connected to conscious learning and accuracy. It is also connected to the idea of involving students in their learning through their intelligence and creativity.

Practice

The first time you try to do something new, you are unlikely to be completely successful. And if you are, it might just be a fluke! The same goes for language learning. Students need an opportunity to practise new items in an organised way until they can get their mouths round the sounds and can understand how what they have just learnt fits in with what they knew before. We shall find a lot of practice techniques in this book; here are a few ideas to begin with.

Choral practice, where all the students repeat something together, is useful for beginners because it gives them a chance to try out something new without being listened to individually. New structures are often presented in dialogues. By repeating the dialogue, students can practise new language as if it were in a real conversation. Drills are highly controlled exercises where the teacher gives a prompt and a student gives a response. For example, you might practise the names of the months and ordinal numbers with a drill like this:

Teacher: March is the third month — Pedro.
Pedro: March is the third month.
Teacher: Right. September — Brigitte.
Brigitte: Er, . . . September is the ninth month.

A certain amount of repetition of the new helps it to become automatically available. However, while this repetition may include some relatively mechanical steps, this must not go on until it becomes boring and mindless. Only the meaningful is memorable.

> So, the sooner practice connects with communication and personal interests, the better.

This strand of ELT is connected to conscious learning and accuracy. It is also connected to the idea of creating a structure in which the learner can feel secure.

Strategies

Here are three ways of thinking about strategies for the language learner (taken from Wenden and Rubin 1987):

- Social strategies, e.g: Go to places where English is used.
- Communication strategies, e.g: Practise these phrases for getting into a discussion:

I'd like to come in there . . .
Can I just make a point here?

- Learning strategies, e.g: When you meet a new word in the foreign language, ask yourself what word it sounds like in your own language, then make a mental picture of the two meanings together. So, when I hear *Tafel* in German, it makes me think of the word *toffee* in English. Then I make a picture of a blackboard made of toffee. This helps me remember the meaning of *Tafel*.

The idea of teaching strategies in ELT is connected to the idea that we can improve our learning if we are more aware of what we are doing, how we are doing it, and what choices are available to us. Conscious learning will improve because of our new focus on how to learn. Subconscious learning will improve because of our extra involvement in what is going on.

> If we act with awareness, our chances of conscious and subconscious learning increase in all areas.

The teaching of strategies and increased awareness is also connected to the idea of helping learners achieve independence.

*This chapter has picked apart five strands of ELT: **communication, feelings, rules, practice** and **strategies**. It is helpful to focus on the different strands in order to understand them better, but we also have to remember that the job of the teacher is to weave all these elements into a whole that is stronger than all the separate strands simply added together.*

Questions and activities

Think about your responses and then discuss them with a colleague.

1 Look at the following exercises and say which of the five strands of ELT you think each one relates to most closely. What experience do you have of such exercises, either as learner or teacher? What are your reactions to them?

Discuss with other students. Which of these ideas will help you speak better English? Put them in order of importance, (1–7).

... repeating new words and expressions lots of times.

... going to an English-speaking country.

... learning a lot of vocabulary.

... watching TV/films in English.

... going to English classes.

... reading in English.

... being corrected a lot.

What other ideas have you got?

Ex. 2.1 (Mohamed and Acklam 1992: 122)

Compare some of these people and things. Use (*not*) *as . . . as . . .* Examples:

I'm as good-looking as a film star.

A Volkswagen is not as quiet as a Rolls-Royce.

I/me   a film star   a Volkswagen
a Rolls-Royce   the President   Bach
an elephant   a cat   Canada
rock music   Kenya   a piano

tall   heavy   good-looking
strong   old   fast   economical
cold   warm   cheap   expensive
big   noisy   quiet   comfortable
intelligent   nice

Ex. 2.2 (Swan and Walter 1990: 67)

In this game **A** shows a sequence of numbers with fingers. **B** says the numbers. **C** writes the numbers down. (*Remember:* **A** does not talk. **C** can't see **A**.)

B   ... three ...   A   C

Ex. 2.3 (Harmer 1988: 76)

Indefinite article
a desk   **an** apple
a pen   **an** orange

Definite article
the pen
the apple

Plurals
(the) pen**s**
(the) apple**s**

When do you use *an*?
What letter makes a word plural?

Ex. 2.4 (Abbs and Freebairn 1990: 10)

<table>
<tr><td>

LEVEL
Elementary +

TIME
30 minutes

MATERIALS
None

PREPARATION
Be prepared to tell a story to the group

</td><td>

BEFORE CLASS

Bring to mind a success story of yours. It can be something very minor like solving a small technical problem or it could be a major life success. Be ready to tell it to the group.

In class

Tell the group your success story. Give them some thinking time and ask them to come up with success stories of their own. Find out how many people have such stories ready to tell. Ask these people to work in small groups with people who have not yet thought of any. Don't pressurise the people who can't recall success stories fast. Once the small groups get going, many students who could not at first remember stories find them coming.

RATIONALE

Even for students who don't like studying languages, it is warming to be asked to speak of their successes in other fields. Focussing on pleasurable things may make even the language class seem more palatable.

NOTES

For a few students, being asked to think about successes brings failures to mind. This is a risk you have to take.

</td></tr>
</table>

Ex. 2.5 (Davis and Rinvolucri 1990: 62)

2 Having established the strand of ELT which each exercise mainly relates to, which other elements can you recognise in the exercises?

3 This chapter suggests that there are two ways in which people learn foreign languages and two overall approaches to teaching them. How closely do these ways of learning and teaching match each other?

4 This chapter suggests that there are two broad approaches to language teaching. In what ways do they relate to the five strands of ELT that are described?

5 Look again at the characteristics of good learners in Chapter 1. How do they relate to the strands of ELT described in this chapter?

The English language

If you look into any classroom, you can expect to see learners and a teacher working. These are the common elements of an educational situation that we have considered so far: people and processes. It is now time to look more closely at the particular focus of the ELT class, the language itself. We begin with the position of English in the world and the relevance of that position to ELT. We then look at some different ways of thinking about what language is, as well as ways of teaching these different aspects of language.

English as an international language

British trade, followed by colonial and imperial expansion, spread English round the world. Since then, the military and economic dominance of the United States of America has confirmed English as the international language of the present historical period. As a consequence, English serves for many people as a bridge into the worlds of higher education, science, international trade, politics, tourism or any other venture which interests them. At the same time, English serves for many times many more people as a barrier between themselves and those same fields of interest. Many people in their own countries will not be able to become doctors, for example, if they cannot learn enough English.

So, we should not contrast 'the ELT classroom' with 'the real world'. The ELT classroom is as real a part of the world as any other. As an English language teacher, you can see yourself as helping people develop their lives, or you can see yourself as supporting a system of world domination, or both. You can also ignore the issue for most of the time, but don't be surprised if it pops up now and again.

The role of English is a large issue, which we can best deal with briefly here in terms of *attitude, ownership,* and *ability.*

Attitude

If people have a positive attitude towards a language and the speakers of that language, this will help them learn the language. In some cases, people might even be learning English because they want to be accepted into an English-speaking society; this is called *integrative* motivation. But a lot of people learn English because they have a goal for themselves which has nothing to do with integration. I remember, for example, teaching English to German engineers who were going to work in Brazil and Argentina. Their motivation was certainly *instrumental*, and it is English as an international language which interests and motivates such learners. Positive attitudes remain important, but now the learners are themselves the users of English about whom they must have a positive attitude. So, who does this language belong to?

Ownership

In many countries, such as India, Nigeria and Singapore, English is widely used in at least some parts of everyday life. This is the situation which is meant when people talk about English as a Second Language. But the issue of ownership goes beyond this to include people from countries where English is certainly a foreign language.

When a Chilean scientist wants to speak to a Chinese scientist, they will probably use English: English is their common language. An international language belongs to its users, not to the countries whose national languages have become internationalised. I am a native speaker of British English, but I am clearly not a native speaker of English as an international language. The idea of a native speaker of an international language is a logical contradiction. When we accept that an international language belongs to its users, we can also see that:

- People who learn an international language are claiming something which naturally belongs to them.
- The important issue is not one of native/non-native speaker as an accident of birth, but of ability to use the language internationally.
- Native speakers of national Englishes (British, American, etc.) are only partners in the international language. They also have to learn communication strategies if they are to use it effectively.

Ability

When we talk about ability, this implies an ability to do something. This something might be to pass an examination, get a job, do a job, write a letter, or make a speech. Acceptable standards of correctness will always be involved in these activities and, as teachers, it is our responsibility to help our students meet those standards.

But we must also have an appropriate idea of what standards are acceptable in different situations. Languages change across time and space, so we can expect different standards and models to develop in an international language. For this reason, we shall prize the ability to be flexible in communication as well as the ability to meet fixed ideas of correctness.

> Being informed about local models of English, local purposes and local needs is part of the job.

These issues of attitude, ownership and ability are especially important in the world of ELT because the great majority of English language teachers have themselves learnt English as a second or foreign language. As such, and given the appropriate level of ability, they serve as the best possible models for their learners.

In the final analysis, you will inevitably spend a lot of time teaching your own English, whatever that is. But inspecting your own attitudes about ownership and ability might help you see where your English fits in with English in the world today.

Aspects of English

When we want to say something, we need to know the *words* that express our meanings and how to put those words together in *grammar* so that they make sense. We want to be sure that the *function* of what we are saying and our *pronunciation* are not only clear, but also appropriate in our *discourse* with other people.

So, our headings here will be: *Words, Grammar, Functions, Pronunciation* and *Discourse*. As we look at these, think about the importance to all of them of what we discussed in Chapter 2: communication, feelings, rules, practice and strategies.

Words

Knowing a lot of words in a foreign language is very important. The more words you know, the better your chance of understanding or making yourself understood. Still, you are always likely to get into situations where your vocabulary is not enough. So, for ELT purposes, we have two important issues:

● How to teach students new words.
● How to teach students what to do when they do not know a word.

How to teach students new words

The more senses you can involve in learning a word, the more likely you are to remember it. So, if someone tells you the name of a fruit just as you have bitten into it, and you are holding it and looking at it, with the taste in your mouth and the smell in your nose, there is a very good chance you will remember that name. Objects and pictures are widely used in language teaching for this reason. When you are teaching, think about how you might use the other senses as well.

We can group words according to what they refer to. Working with these *lexical sets* can help people learn new words:

---

1 With another student, put the words below into these different groups.

1 breakfast food and drink	4 family members
2 numbers	5 continents and countries
3 days of the week	6 interests

tea	father	reading	twenty-five	coffee
ham	Monday	sport	hot chocolate	Sunday
cheese	Europe	music	grandmother	two
baby	sugar	toast	Thursday	films
son	Friday	daughter	Wednesday	seventy
butter	eggs	eight	Australia	brother
Asia	Africa	forty-five	Greece	France

2 Add other words you know to each group.

Ex. 3.1 (Mohamed and Acklam 1992: 32)

Choose topics to work on which relate to your students' outside interests. This is not only motivating in a general way; you will be surprised by the broad vocabulary that some individuals have in their own areas of interest, even those students who might be generally weak. Also, working in an area of interest leads people to want to express their thoughts, which generates a need to learn.

Students can help develop their own lexical sets by exploring their own associations. Try to expand a mind-map for yourself in a foreign language. Where you do not know the foreign language word, write the word in your own best language. As a serious learner, you could go on to look up those words and write them in the target language. Here is my attempt in Spanish, beginning from the central word, *coche*, which means car.

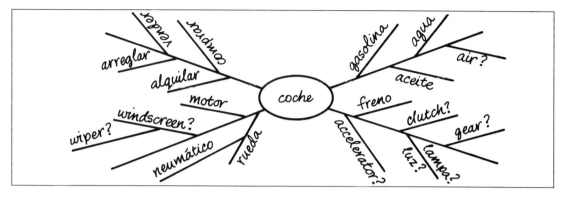

Encourage students to ask for words when they want to express themselves. Encourage them to ask you and to ask each other.

Encourage students to keep their own vocabulary notebooks. They can note down words that they hear or see which they want to remember. They can also write down English words which they meet and simply do not understand, or words in their own language which they wanted to use but did not know the English for. In these last two cases, they can ask, or look them up later and write in the meanings. Tell them that in all cases, it will be much more helpful if they write down enough of a sentence to remind them of exactly how the word is used.

Many students find word cards useful. On one side, you write the word you want to learn; on the other side, a translation, definition, or example which shows the meaning. This last idea is probably the best. The cards can be carried round and looked at at any time.

| *ratty* | *in a bad mood*
'OK, don't get ratty with me! It's not my fault!' |

In Chapter 2 (p. 22), we looked at a memory technique for new words. That strategy uses sound, image, personal associations and individual imagination. Like all strategies, it will suit some people and not others. Some people already use conscious strategies; some people become aware of their strategies only when asked. Do get students to talk about the strategies they use.

> The more aware learners become of possible strategies, the more chance they have of discovering something helpful to themselves.

How to teach students what to do when they do not know a word

As we have said, words are very important. But that is not the same as saying that every single word in every larty sentence has to be understood. Students often stop reading or listening because they meet an unfamiliar word, or they give up trying to express themselves because they can't think of the exact word they want.

As far as reading and listening are concerned, teach the following approach to unknown words:

1 Ignore them and carry on. Most probably the meaning will become clear, or it was not important.

2 Later on, if you still want to know what a word means, try to work the meaning out. You can use clues:
   - from your own language – is there a word with a common root (a *cognate*)? This is a strategy that can get you into trouble. The German *nervös*, for example, is much closer in meaning to the English word *irritable* than to *nervous*. Nevertheless, guessing a meaning based on the recognition of a cognate is more likely to be a help than a hindrance.
   - from the structure of the word – is it like another English word? If you know the word *rely*, you can guess the meanings of *reliable* and *reliability*. As you recognise the significance of the endings, *-able* and *-ity* in making adjectives and nouns, you can also transfer this knowledge to good use in working out the meanings of other words.
   - from the context – What do you think the (nonsense) word *larty* means in the first paragraph of this section? How important is it to have a one-word equivalent?

3 If you are not satisfied with the meaning you work out, ask someone, or use a dictionary.

- Make sure that even from the most elementary level, students know how to ask, 'What does . . . mean?'
- Teaching students to use a dictionary is an important part of the job. The more advanced they are, the more benefit they can get from a monolingual learner's dictionary. These contain a lot of information about the language and can be a great source of independent learning. Remember that some students might not have learnt dictionary skills in their first language, that some languages are not alphabetical, and that there are alphabets other than the roman: take nothing for granted! Here is an exercise for helping students learn how to use a dictionary.

IRREGULAR PLURALS

Most nouns make their plural forms by adding **-s** or **-es**. If a word has an irregular plural, the dictionary shows you the correct form.

po·ta·to /pə'teɪtəʊ/ n **potatoes** [C;U] a round white vegetable with a thin brown or yellow skin, that is cooked and served in many different ways: *I've peeled the potatoes.* | *baked potatoes* | *Is there any mashed potato left?*

Exercise 11*
Write the correct plural form of these words:

abacus	....	**cargo**	....
grouse	....	**index**	....
phenomenon	....	**sky**	....
tomato	....	**wife**	....

Ex. 3.2 (Longman Active Study Dictionary 1991: 13)

Where students use bilingual dictionaries, especially small ones, show them how to look up a word in one direction (e.g: Spanish → English) and then check it in the other direction to make sure it is the meaning they want.

As far as speaking and writing are concerned, it is important to be able to ask for meanings in English. Teach expressions such as 'What's the English for . . . ?' or 'How do you say . . . in English?' right at the beginning.

It is also important to develop the ability to say what you want to in another way. Three useful expressions to teach early on are:
- you know   a phrase for filling a pause and signalling that you want your listener to cooperate; see examples below:

- a thing (for) for avoiding unknown nouns, e.g:
  Have you got — you know, a thing for lifting the car?
- when you for avoiding unknown verbs, e.g:
  I want to — you know, when you put the eggs in oil . . .

Note that we set out to consider how to teach words, but a great deal of the discussion has been about how to learn words.

> A lot of the teacher's work is done in raising the learners' awareness of how to learn.

Grammar

There is no completely satisfactory way of describing the grammar of any language. We use grammatical terms, such as *noun, verb, adjective, adverb, preposition, article,* etc., because they help us talk about the language as we try to understand, and help others understand, how it works.

Similarly, we make grammatical generalisations as they seem useful to learners. We tell them 'Don't use an infinitive after *suggest*' because we know that '*Michael suggested to leave the party*' is a common mistake.

We may tell them 'Here, use *some* in positive sentences and *any* in negative sentences and questions' because that generalisation will help them with a lot of the straightforward utterances that they want to make at an early stage. But students need to understand that they can make better rules as they learn more, and teachers need to know enough grammar to be able to respond satisfactorily when a student asks about sentences such as 'Do you want some coffee?' and 'Please take any of them.'

If you grew up in English, you may never have studied the grammar of the language. If you want to be an English language teacher, however, you need to do so now. Without grammatical awareness, you may be able to slip through awkward situations on the basis of your fluency and insight, but you will not be in a position to give your students the help that they need.

If you have learnt English as a foreign language yourself, you probably have a good grasp of the basics of English grammar, as well as an insight into what your learners may find difficult. Nevertheless, you will not be able to answer all the questions that you are asked. So, there are two things just as important for a teacher as having a sound knowledge of grammar:

> You have to be able to admit that you don't know something.

> You have to be able to find the answer that you didn't know.

If you grew up in English, it is quite easy to say, 'I don't know, I'll look it up.' Then you have to make sure that you do so, and explain what you find to your students. As they advance, it is worth spending time showing them how they can look things up themselves.

If you have learnt English as a foreign or second language, it is more difficult to say 'I don't know,' because it attacks your confidence and you worry about what the students will think. But as *nobody* knows the whole of a grammar, you really have to decide if you are going to:

- base your confidence on a pretence of knowing, or
- base your confidence on an ability to look things up and explain.

Teaching the grammar of the language takes up a great deal of ELT, particularly in the early stages, and we shall return to the topic at some length in Chapters 7 and 8. Before we finish this section, however, let us think again about our five strands of ELT and grammar teaching. The importance of rules and practice should be obvious, and learning how to use a grammar book is an important strategy that we have mentioned.

We also have to remember the importance of communication and personal feelings in ELT when we are teaching grammar. Here is a simple activity to practise the Past Simple, while also contrasting it with the Present Perfect.

1 Teacher writes on the board a list of adjectives such as: *frightened, surprised, overjoyed, angry, delighted, relieved.*
2 Students work in pairs.
   Student A chooses an adjective and asks:
   'Have you ever felt really . . . ?'
   Student B thinks about it and replies:
   'Yes, I have.' or 'No, I haven't.'
3 If the answer is 'No', Student A asks again with a different adjective.
4 If the answer is 'Yes', Student A asks, 'What happened?'
5 Student B tells the story.
6 The students change roles.

You could follow this up with Question 3 at the end of this chapter.

Functions

In our discussion of communication in Chapter 2, we talked about the importance of:

- getting a message across, and
- getting things done.

The idea of teaching *functions* in ELT has arisen from the second of these concerns. When we *say* something, we also *do* something; when we use grammatical structures, we also carry out language functions. Here are some examples to make this clear:

Saying this		Doing this
'I'm sorry.'	*usually 'means'*	Apologising
'Can you come to dinner next week?'		Inviting
'There's a car coming!'		Warning

Unfortunately, there is no simple way of relating functions to each other, nor of relating them to grammatical structures, but the use of functions in ELT is helpful in the following ways:

1 From the student's point of view, it is motivating to learn to do things in a language rather than just learn structures.

2 The teacher can use a function in order to give a context for the teaching of a structure. For example, you might encourage the use of student imagination and humour by practising the conditional structure, *If + Present Simple, will + Verb Stem* in the context of the function *threaten*:

> Think of ten different ways of completing the final sentence below. There will be a prize for the funniest.
>
> *You are sitting in the cinema and the man behind you keeps tapping your seat with his foot. Twice you ask him to stop. Twice he starts again. You turn round and say, 'Look, if you do that again, I'll . . . .'*

This is particularly useful for students who have previously been taught in a straightforward structural fashion, because it allows you to go over old ground in a new way.

3 Concentrating on functions gives a chance to deal with the difficult matter of appropriacy that we mentioned in Chapter 2. All the following ways of 'inviting' are correct, and all might be said fluently. The important thing is to choose the appropriate one for the person you are talking to:

'Do you fancy dinner on Saturday?'
'Could I invite you to dinner on Saturday?'
'I was wondering if you might be free for dinner on Saturday?'

Here is an exercise which teaches this kind of point:

⟦⊚ⓒ⟧ **Match the questions and answers. You can find more than one answer to each question.**

QUESTIONS
1. Sorry to trouble you, but could you lend me some bread?
2. Could you lend me a dictionary?
3. Could you show me some black sweaters, please?
4. Excuse me. Have you got a light, please?
5. Could you possibly lend me your car for half an hour?
6. Could I borrow your keys for a moment?
7. Could I borrow your umbrella, please?
8. Have you got a cigarette?

ANSWERS
a. I think so . . . Yes, here you are.
b. Yes, of course. Just a minute.
c. I'm sorry. I need it/them.
d. I'm afraid I haven't got one.
e. I'm afraid I haven't got any.
f. Sorry, I don't smoke.
g. I'm sorry, I'm afraid I can't.

Look at the questions again; find two very polite questions and two very casual questions.

Ex. 3.3 (Swan and Walter 1990: 85)

4 If a group of students is learning English for a particular purpose, whether occupational (they are all waiters), or academic (they are all students of Chemistry), you can make a list of things that they need to be able to do with the language. This type of approach, called *English for Specific Purposes* (ESP), has become a major component of ELT worldwide.

Pronunciation

The three most important elements of pronunciation for ELT are:

- Stress — which words, or which parts of a word, you say loudest and longest;
- Intonation — the way your voice goes up and/or down as you speak, especially at the end of what you say;
- Sounds — as in the separate sounds of *pen*: /p/, /e/, /n/.

Stress

In dictionaries, word stress is usually marked with a small line just before the stressed syllable, e.g: 'record, re'cord. Notice the grammatical difference that the stress marks here. It is certainly worth using exercises like this one to make sure that your students can actually hear different stress in words:

▣ SPEECHWORK

Listen and underline the stressed syllable.

beautiful   interesting   industrial   gallery
historical   restaurant   cathedral   university

Ex. 3.4 (Abbs and Freebairn 1990: 28)

Sentence stress is important for two reasons. First, the rhythm of English speech tends to bounce along from stressed syllable to stressed syllable with the same amount of time between the stresses, no matter how many unstressed syllables intervene. If you say, 'This is a TERRibly obSCURE POINT!' and tap out the rhythm of the stresses, you will find that the amount of time between 'SCURE' and 'POINT' is the same as that taken to say the three syllables of 'ib-ly-ob'. And you will also notice that 'This is a' is said very quickly in order to rush on to the first stressed syllable.

All this seems very natural to a person who has grown up speaking English, but it may well not be to the learner. In fact, this is a major reason why many people say that English speakers talk very quickly, or swallow their words, or mumble. The language teacher can help by doing what you just did, providing a rhythm by tapping on the desk, or clapping hands, especially when students are practising a new language structure.

The second reason why stress is so vital is that we clearly stress words which we think are important to the meaning of what we want to say. Try saying this simple sentence in three different ways, each time stressing a different part: I'll help you.

What different situations come to mind as you say the sentence differently? What other changes take place in the rise and fall of your voice as you stress different words? As you can see, stress and intonation carry a lot of information.

Intonation

We have seen that intonation can change the meaning of what is said. Intonation is also closely related to politeness, and therefore to appropriacy. In normal speech outside the classroom, people will overlook grammatical inaccuracy and hesitancy, but if they feel that someone is being impolite, they are not so forgiving. Look back to the requests in Ex. 3.3 and notice how important intonation is. What impression might you give if you used the wrong intonation?

As with grammar, people do not want to learn about rules of stress and intonation for their own sake. They want to be able to use stress and intonation meaningfully. For this reason, the teacher has to keep them constantly in mind when teaching other things.

> Even if the students are only repeating a dialogue, or
> practising new structures in a drill, or using functions in
> an exercise, insist that they say their lines meaningfully.

The teacher can also use *feelings* to help students in areas such as tone and pitch, where it is very difficult to state any rules, or even provide any clear descriptions of what is happening. When, for instance, the students have completed an exercise practising some point of grammar, the teacher might say:

Who can do number three again? This time say it as if you are surprised. Now number eight – as though you didn't mean it.

Sounds

The separate sounds of a language which can make a difference in meaning are called *phonemes*. If we substitute the phoneme /t/ for the phoneme /p/ in the word *pen*, we get *ten*; if we substitute the phoneme /k/ for /f/, we change the word *phone* to *cone*.

This *phonemic transcription* is written between oblique lines /laɪk ðɪs/. The attraction of the system is that we have one written symbol for each sound of spoken English, without the complications of standard English spelling. This is the International Phonetic Alphabet (IPA) as it is used for standard British English and standard American English.

CONSONANTS		VOWELS	
Symbol	Key Word	Symbol	Key Word
p	**p**ack	e	b**e**d
b	**b**ack	æ	b**a**d
t	**t**ie	iː	sh**ee**p
d	**d**ie	ɪ	sh**i**p
k	**c**lass	ɑː	c**a**lm
g	**g**lass	ɒ	p**o**t
		ɔː	c**au**ght, h**or**se
tʃ	**ch**ur**ch**	ʊ	p**u**t
dʒ	**j**u**dg**e	uː	b**oo**t
		ʌ	c**u**t
f	**f**ew	ɜː	b**ir**d
v	**v**iew	ə	bett**er**
θ	**th**row		
ð	**th**ough	eɪ	m**a**ke
s	**s**oon	əʊ	b**oa**t
z	**z**oo	aɪ	b**i**te
ʃ	**sh**oe	aʊ	n**ow**
ʒ	mea**s**ure	ɔɪ	b**oy**
		ɪə	h**ere**
m	su**m**	eə	h**air**
n	su**n**	ʊə	p**oor**
ŋ	su**ng**		
		eɪə	pl**ayer**
h	**h**ot	əʊə	l**ower**
l	**l**ot	ɔɪə	empl**oyer**
r	**r**od	aɪə	t**ire**
j	**y**et	aʊə	fl**ower**
w	**w**et		

For your own purposes as a teacher, a familiarity with this alphabet can be helpful in at least four ways:

- It shows you what separate sounds are involved in standard English. This kind of knowledge increases confidence.
- You may discover that your own pronunciation differs from the standard in some places, as mine does. When I am challenged by a student about a difference between my pronunciation and the pronunciation on a tape I have played, I can acknowledge this and explain exactly what the difference is. I explain that I *can* make the standard sound if I think about it, but in my normal speech, I don't. In other words, differences between the teacher's English and standard English should not be a threat as long as you can show that you know what is going on.
- Any good dictionary will give a pronunciation guide in an alphabet similar to the one above. This is important, because we all meet words in our reading which we do not know how to pronounce. For me, the last time this happened was with the word *chimera*, which I now know is pronounced /kaɪˈmiːərə/.
- While you might not know all the symbols by heart, the fact that you know how to use the alphabet to demonstrate a difference or look up a pronunciation gives you a skill you can feel good about.

Teachers disagree about the usefulness of teaching such an alphabet to language learners. Some people argue that students have enough problems without learning a strange new alphabet, and that teaching such an alphabet is too academic for an ELT class. Others say that learning this alphabet will help students become independent learners, able to develop the skills that we have just listed above, based on their own increased awareness. While you make up your own mind what will best suit your students, here are two techniques which do employ the IPA.

- When training students to use a dictionary, it is worth spending time showing them how the alphabet works and giving them some practice in working out unfamiliar pronunciations. You can then respond to further inquiries as they arise, and students who want to develop this skill will have the chance to do so.
- Isolate certain sounds in English which cause trouble for your students. Do they, perhaps, often confuse /ɔ:/ and /əʊ/, so that the words *caught* and *coat* are pronounced identically? Put these two symbols on the wall with typical words under each one. When the mistake occurs at a time suitable for immediate correction, you merely point to one list or the other. After a while, you can take the example words away and just use the symbols.

In the area of pronunciation in general, there is very little to explain. Most of the work has to be done by listening and practice, by helping students develop a 'good ear'. In so doing, look out for the opportunity to use models other than yourself, so that your students get used to a variety of pronunciation. When a student says something well, use that student as a model and encourage everyone to listen carefully.

In everyday work, there are two points to keep in mind:

- Make the teaching of pronunciation a constant element of the rest of your teaching. (Look at the materials on p. 67 for an example of how highlighting stress can support the learning of grammar and communicative ability. Notice, too, the use of the IPA.)
- Give short but regular bursts of treatment to aspects of pronunciation that seem particularly important for your students.

Discourse

By discourse, we mean language in use. A lot of what we said about communication in Chapter 2, and about functions in this chapter is relevant here. The two most important aspects of language which are dealt with under this heading are:

- How do people use language to interact with each other?
- How is language organised beyond the grammar of the sentence?

Here is an ELT activity aimed at practising structured interaction according to a framework of how a discourse might develop:

Making dialogues

Make dialogues using the cues in brackets. Do *not* use the words in *italics* in your dialogues. When asking questions, use either direct or less direct questions.

a) A is a shop assistant. B is a customer.
   A: (Greet. Offer to help.)
   B: (Politely ask for your money back for a necklace you bought. Give a reason.)
   A: (Refuse. Explain why not.)
   B: (Respond in any way you like.)

Ex. 3.5 (Bell and Gower 1991: 143)

The rules of grammar extend only to the description of sentences, but we can see that language in use is regularly organised beyond those boundaries. We can see that sentences are 'joined together' in different ways. They are, for example, linked by the use of pronouns, by logical relationships, and by the repetition of words. Let us look more closely at the last two sentences.

The expression 'different ways' in the first sentence signals to the reader that at least two of these 'ways' are about to be listed. The expression 'for example' in the second sentence confirms the relationship of Statement – Example which organises this tiny discourse of two sentences. The pronoun 'They' in the second sentence refers back to 'sentences' in the first. The words 'joined together' are repeated in the form of the paraphrase 'linked'.

Here is a typical ELT exercise focusing on this area of language:

Into the mouth of the volcano

In 1986 Shell Sanders, a young American, arrived in Sumatra, an island in Indonesia, to climb one of the active volcanoes.

(As soon as) he got there he tried to find a guide (but,) unfortunately, the only guide was out of town. Although it was a dangerous climb, Shell decided to go up alone. Before he left, Shell said goodbye to Esther, the manager of his hotel.

When he got to the top of the 9,000 foot volcano there was fog everywhere. While he was looking down 120 feet into the mouth of the volcano, he fell in and nearly killed himself.

Four days later, when her guest didn't return, Esther realised she must do something. However, she didn't know who to ask. Finally, she asked a local man to help. The man communicated with spirits, who told her where Shell was. He said that, as well as broken bones, he had bad spirits inside him, too.

Eventually, the police found the injured man and took him to hospital.

2 *As soon as* and *but* are linking expressions. Circle eleven other linking expressions in the text. List them in the columns below according to whether they add extra information (*addition*), indicate when something happened (*time*), or contrast facts (*contrast*).

ADDITION	TIME	CONTRAST
	as soon as	*but*

Ex. 3.6 (Bell and Gower 1991: 24)

*In this chapter, we have thought about ELT as an international activity, and have looked in some detail at what a language is made up of: **words**, which we **pronounce** and bring together in **grammar** in order to **function** in our **discourse** with other people.*

Questions and activities

Think about your responses and then discuss them with a colleague.

1 Does English really belong to an international community? Or does it really belong to those people who grew up as native speakers of English?

2 Do you have a favourite way of remembering words? Ask others and find at least one different strategy that you can try out.

3 If you intend to go on with this interest in ELT, you should own a reference grammar. Spend some time getting to know it. What does it tell you about the difference between the form and function of the Present Perfect and the Past Simple? How does that information relate to the activity on page 33?

4 While it is true that none of us can explain all the rules of English grammar, we can all keep learning, and there is a bare minimum of grammatical knowledge which we need to have. The following are terms you might expect to find in a beginners' course. If you are not comfortable about using them, check them in your reference grammar.

adjective	infinitive	preposition
adverb	interrogative	present perfect
article	irregular verb	present progressive
auxiliary verb	modal verb	present simple
comparative	negative	quantifier
conditional clause	noun	question
countable noun	participle	reported speech
declarative	past progressive	short form
demonstrative	past simple	stem
direct object	pronoun	tag
imperative	plural	tense
indirect object	possessive	verb

5 Make a list of functions for yourself. Write down different ways of carrying out those functions in English, or in any other language. What would lead you to choose one way rather than another?

6 Choose any short text. Can you see ways in which the text is linked together, so that it is more than just a series of separate sentences?

4 Materials

As we said at the beginning of the last chapter, when you look into an ELT classroom, you expect to see learners and a teacher doing things in English. What you will also expect to see are some teaching materials, and they are the focus of this chapter.

When you begin teaching, you will probably be given a textbook. You can also probably depend on the fact that you will be expected to be able to *use* a textbook. At this point, it is reasonable to ask, 'How do I teach these materials?', and that is a question which this book constantly tries to answer. But there is a danger in this question which some teachers never escape. They try to fit themselves and their students into the demands made by their materials.

Materials exist in order to support learning and teaching, so they should be designed to suit the people and the processes involved. Where this is not the case, it is the materials, or the use of them, which need to change.

> Our purpose is not to teach materials. Our purpose is to teach students, and to use materials in that process.

There is one more general point to be made:

> Use your materials with enthusiasm.

If you think you should be using different materials, then do something about it before the next class, but don't poison this lesson's learning opportunities. A negative attitude from the teacher towards the materials is strongly demotivating for the learners; it takes away their feelings of security and purpose.

Remember that you are there to help the students learn and that students learn in many different ways. Certainly, some materials are better than others, but just about any type of material can be used well by a committed teacher.

In this chapter, we shall look at *published materials, teacher-produced materials, student materials* and *authentic materials.*

Published materials

In this section, I refer explicitly to textbooks and coursebooks. I mean my comments to apply also to the huge range of supplementary books, mostly focusing on particular types of classroom activity, or on specific language skills, which are available in ELT.

Publishing ELT materials is big business, and it arouses strong feelings. Some teachers are as fiercely against textbooks as others are in their favour. The pity of it is that some teachers on both sides of the argument simply follow books instead of using them. And some teachers pour massive amounts of time and energy into producing a poor quality, home-made version of what is already available. Then they are often disappointed by the reaction of their students, who prefer the appeal and authority of a good textbook.

As long as we remember that we are teaching students, not materials, we can usually use published materials, and then use our energy and creativity in areas where it is more needed. So, it is important to develop a clear idea of what you can expect published materials to do for you, and what they cannot do.

When you are given a published textbook to use, you should be able to expect that a great deal of effort has gone into making it:

- *attractive* – in terms of topics, layout and illustrations. You have to check this with students, of course; what is attractive in one context may not be in another.
- *reliable* – in terms of the overall choice and sequencing of what is taught, the correctness of information, and the dependability of the exercises and activities. You have to check this, too: mistakes will creep into any text.
- *user-friendly* – in that at least one way of using the materials is clear to teacher and students, giving both of them security for classwork and homework. Wherever possible, get a copy of the teacher's book, which will give you other options to consider in the use of the materials.

Let us look at two typical exercises in this light:

Look at the pictures.

Pat is wearing a white sweater, a green blouse, and a red and black skirt.

Make some more sentences about Keith, Annie and Robert.

'Keith is wearing . . .'

Ex. 4.1 (Swan and Walter 1990: 45)

We have a simple but attractive drawing (originally in colour) of a mixed gender, mixed race group of people. We can assume that the learning of this type of vocabulary about clothes, and the practice of the Present Progressive tense to describe people's appearance fit reasonably well into the learning progression of a book designed for this level of student. The book gives us a model to follow, then a clear instruction, then an example to complete.

Here, we have a clearly drawn map and listening tasks. Having understood the directions functionally, students are led to focus their attention on the language itself. They then work in pairs on using this new language in a similar but different way to how they heard it. The book makes clear how the material can be used.

1 ▣ **Listen to Jon and Neesha talking on the telephone and answer these questions.**

1 Why is she phoning him?
2 When is she going to his house?

2 **Mark the route from Neesha's house to Jon's house on the map.**

Vocabulary: street directions

1 ▣ **Listen again and complete the sentences.**

Go . . . Castle Avenue.
Turn . . . Brick Street.
Go straight . . ., . . . the pub.
Turn . . .
Go . . . Market Road . . . the traffic lights.
Go . . . the traffic lights.
Take the second road . . . the right.

2 **Work with another student. Write the directions from Jon's house to Neesha's house.**

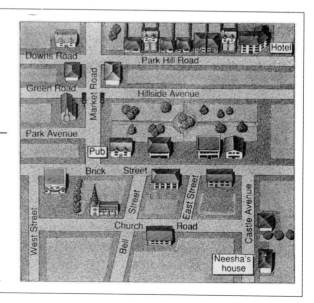

Ex. 4.2 (Mohamed and Acklam 1992: 97)

Now let's turn to what a published textbook cannot provide:

- *insight* – into the interests and needs of any specific students;
- *decisions* – about which materials to use, and which to change, supplement, or leave out;
- *creativity* – to use the materials as the foundations of a bridge which students cross as they learn to speak for themselves.

These elements must, of course, be supplied by the teacher. This is just one of the areas where method and materials overlap, but let us look first of all at the role of teacher-produced materials.

Teacher-produced materials

In most teaching situations, the most important role of teacher-produced materials is to bridge the gap between the classroom and the world outside.

So, the teacher might produce a map similar to Ex. 4.2 above which represents the area around the school where the class takes place, or a well-known area of the local city. The same exercise can then be done in local terms. If the students are in need of lots of practice, the teacher-produced exercise can follow the one in the textbook. If less practice is needed, the localised material might replace the exercise in the textbook. In either case, the result should be that:

- the use of English is related to the world outside the classroom;
- there is authentic communication between the learners.

Until and unless you become very skilled at materials production, with resources and facilities to back you up, perhaps the most useful materials production you can do is this type of extension of given exercises into the students' own place and time, engaging their imagination, their intelligence, their sense of humour (you know how the list goes on . . .).

Another important task is to introduce what are called *authentic materials* into the classroom.

Authentic materials

The word *authentic* is used in different ways in ELT, but the most common use of the expression *authentic materials* is to refer to examples of language that were not originally produced for language learning purposes but which are now being used in that way. So, if you decided to cut an article out of a newspaper and use it in class, this would be an example of authentic material. Authentic materials are most usually reading texts, sometimes listening texts.

There are two reasons why authentic materials are so important:

- *Language* – Authentic materials represent the actual goal of language learning, including the difficulties that learning materials avoid. All learners must have practice in meeting these real challenges. Even at the early stages, students should learn how to respond to language which they do not fully understand.
- *Motivation* – Authentic materials bring the means of learning and the purpose of learning close together, and this establishes once again a direct link with the world outside the classroom.

One way to use authentic materials is to take the exercises and frameworks you find with other materials and use them with your own.

Here are two general exercises which work well with appropriate texts and which train useful skills in reading and listening:

> E.g. 1 As you read the text, put a tick (✓) in the margin if you agree with the writer and a cross (✗) if you disagree. Afterwards, discuss your ticks and crosses with a partner.

> E.g. 2 What problem is the speaker discussing? What solutions have been tried? What was wrong with them? What solution does the speaker suggest?

These ideas about making materials local and authentic are also at the heart of what I mean by *student materials*.

Student materials

The examples of student materials I give here actually come from the same textbooks as the sample exercises themselves. These writers recognise that their books are only there to begin the language learning process which the teacher must link up with the lives of the students. Not all textbooks are so helpful.

We can think of student materials in two ways:

- learning materials produced by the students;
- the students themselves as materials.

Student-produced materials

As a follow-up to Ex. 4.2 you can ask the students to produce simple
maps of an area that they know as the basis for an activity of the
same type. The students are then using their own knowledge and
personal backgrounds to produce learning materials for their
classmates. In addition to the effects noted under teacher-produced
materials, the learners also have a *personal* investment in the
materials. That is to say, they have put their own background,
knowledge and creativity into the material and they will be
interested in what comes out of it.

Students as materials

Ex. 4.1 gives everyone in the class a place to begin, but the really
useful work depends on what happens next. The classroom contains
real people wearing their clothes, and this can be the basis of
extended practice. We thus make sure that students are learning
words that are directly relevant to their lives. For example, the class
might be wearing a selection of sandals, sneakers, trainers and
thongs on their feet. It is not the textbook writer's business to know
this; it is the teacher's business to make the connections.

When we see the learners as materials, we can also use our methods
to make learning enjoyable. We could, for instance:

- Ask a student to close his or her eyes and describe what someone
  else is wearing.
- Ask a student to describe what someone else is wearing until the
  rest of us can recognise that person.
- Divide the class into pairs and ask each pair to do one of the above.

In such ways, we can ensure that:

- the use of English is related to the world of the classroom;
- there is authentic communication by and about the learners.

Students, of course, only follow a textbook once, whereas teachers
may use the same book several times.

> Relating to the lives of the students isn't only good for the
> learning process, it also brings in variety and freshness for
> the teacher.

The smaller the group of students you have, the easier it often
becomes to encourage genuine personalisation of the learning process.

If you are working on a one-to-one basis, the learner's personal and professional environment becomes your content material, and teaching is a kind of supportive pairwork which helps the learner live in that environment in English.

This chapter has shown how published materials are often useful as a reliable basis, onto which teachers can build locally relevant materials arising from authentic texts and their students' own lives.

Questions and activities

Think about your responses and then discuss them with a colleague.

1   What is your experience of teaching or being taught a language from:
    ● a textbook?
    ● teacher-produced materials?
    ● student-produced materials?

2   Look at any textbook or textbooks that you can find.
    ● Are they attractive and user-friendly?
    ● If you look at some parts in detail, do they seem reliable?
    ● Do the books themselves help you localise the work they introduce?

3   Look at a piece of material in a student's coursebook and try to think of different ways of teaching it. Then check the teacher's book and see if there are any different ideas there. Repeat this for different books.

4   Look at some textbook exercises and think about how you might:
    ● produce material to relate the work to a particular class;
    ● get the students to produce a piece of related material;
    ● organise an activity to draw on the students' appearance, knowledge, background, etc. as material;
    ● organise an activity in which the students really communicate with each other about themselves.

5   What is your experience of teaching or being taught a foreign language with authentic materials? Find an authentic text with which you could use one of the general exercises on p. 47.

Environment and equipment

Almost all classes take place in a room with furniture in it. This setting gives shape to the physical and psychological environment in which students and teachers work, and that is where we are going to start this chapter. We shall then look at the most basic piece of classroom equipment, the board. Finally, we shall make some brief comments on those items of teaching technology which can either help us or get in the way: the overhead projector, the audiocassette player and the videocassette player.

The room

We can think about a classroom in the following terms:

- Size – Is it big enough for students to sit and move around in without being so big that you feel you are only camping in part of it?
- Shape – Can everyone see the board or screen, and can you see all the students?
- Light – Can everyone see well enough to read and write without having light reflected on the board or screen?
- Environment – Can you regulate the temperature? Is the room clean? Is it attractive? Is it supportive to learning?
- Noise – Is it quiet enough for everyone to be heard, but not placed so that people will complain when all your students talk at once?

If your room is unsatisfactory in any of these ways, ask yourself the basic question, 'Does it have to be like this?' You can't change the size of a room, but you might ask if another room is available. If all the classroom walls are bare, perhaps that is because no one ever asked if they could put up posters, or display student writing. Is there some way of sticking things on the walls without marking them? If so, always carry a bit of this adhesive with you.

Perhaps teachers of other subjects don't want to work in a room with English language posters or articles from English language magazines on the wall. So, might it be possible in future to timetable one room for English classes all the time, or almost all the time?

> Ensuring a secure, pleasant and interesting place to work is one good step towards successful teaching.

Some things you can change, and some things you can't; your responsibility is to find out the difference between the two without upsetting anyone. Once you have done what you can towards creating a suitable environment for your English-using community, concentrate on being positive about what you have.

Furniture

Furniture sends its own messages. Many living rooms are arranged so that all chairs face the television: the message is that the television dominates much of the time that these families spend in their living rooms. Many classrooms are arranged so that all students face forward to the teacher; the message is clear:

- the teacher dominates;
- all information will come from the teacher;
- interaction between or among students is less valued.

Because the language class is concerned with communication and a variety of interactions, we want our furniture to send a different message. I consider this to be a good, general seating arrangement:

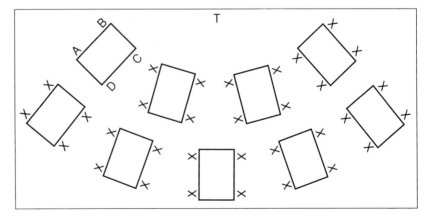

Here, everyone can look towards the front of the class when necessary, and everyone has a table to write on. If cooperative pairwork is needed, A and B can work together. If divided information pairwork is needed, A and D can work together. If groupwork is needed, A, B, C, and D can work together. All of this is possible without anyone having to move. The message is that we are flexible, and that we will work and communicate with different people.

If I want a class to talk about a topic all together, I try to get the tables out of the way. The message is that we are open to each other.

It takes an effort to get students used to the idea of moving furniture, but with time it can be done efficiently, and a little physical movement in our classes can form a natural and useful mini-break in concentration.

There may be pressure on you from colleagues and cleaners to put furniture back into neat rows after your class. In my own country, my response is to ask cleaners to clean the room and leave the furniture where they find it. I tell my colleagues that I will happily leave furniture the way the next teacher wants it as long as the previous teacher leaves it the way I want it. When I was younger, I also used to ask colleagues what it was about students in lines looking at the back of each other's heads that they found so helpful to learning. These are not necessarily good responses! You must learn to be politely assertive in your own way.

In someone else's country, I have always thought it worth the effort to move the furniture back at the end of the class to how people think it 'should' be. I would also invite those people to my lessons to show them why I took the trouble to move it in the first place.

The fact that teachers, administrators and cleaners can get very excited about the way that furniture looks in a room serves to underline the basic point:

> Furniture is not neutral. If you don't use the furniture to conscious effect, it will quietly exercise its own effect.

In some classrooms, the furniture is fixed in place. The best way to get students into groups is often to have two turn round to work with a pair sitting behind them.

The message is: we are not fixed into set positions, even if the furniture is. Each room sets its own challenge. You can ignore it, but you can't make it go away.

Before we leave this topic, let's remind ourselves of the importance of communication in what we hope will become a small English-using community:

> If you can make all this movement and organisation happen by using English, you are doing an important part of the job.

The board

Spend a little time practising your board writing. It's a new skill at which everyone can be competent. Remember that, like any kind of writing, this is a form of communication. Go to the back of the room and check that your writing is big enough, legible and straight.

If you want to have a lot of writing on the board to use in a lesson, see if the room is free beforehand and do the writing then. It's true that this takes up your time, but it gives you a good, relaxed feeling for the lesson, which is usually a fair reward. It also sets up a good atmosphere if your students find you there working for them as they arrive. When you are using the board in front of students, don't let that fact pressure you into scribbling, or not thinking about which part of the board you are writing on.

This last point is important in terms of planning how you will use the board. The great characteristic of the board is that you can rub things out. Unfortunately, this sometimes leads teachers to write something in the middle of the board, then rub it out to make room for something else, then wish they had the first thing back again. One basic strategy is to have different parts of the board for different things. If you keep in mind that you will always reserve the right-hand half of the board for the work you have planned, a left-hand column for new words which come up during the lesson, and the space in between for impromptu examples, diagrams, or whatever, at least you have established some order to help you and your class communicate via the board.

Don't be possessive about the board. Encourage students to use it, too. For example, you might have a reading class with a text about marriage. You could start the lesson by saying, 'Come and write on the board the first word you think of when I say, *Marriage*.' What would you get from this?

- Movement round the classroom – so this technique might be useful in a situation where the students have been sitting for a while.
- Involvement – the students are contributing to the lesson, although they may not yet know how.
- Engagement – the students are giving a personal reaction which will also start them thinking about the topic; this preparatory thinking will ease their way into understanding the passage.
- Skills – one way to start work on the passage would be to have students scan it in order to find ten of the blackboard words in the passage.

On another occasion, a student might ask, 'How do you pronounce this word?' A useful thing for him or her to do is to write it on the board, over on the left where the new words go. Or you might have collected a few errors which students have made in their writing and you can ask a student to write them on the board while you do something else. Or if there is some kind of competition, let there be one or two students at the board keeping score. If, during breaktime, students think of something they wish they could say in English, have them write it on the board in order to remind them to ask you.

> In short, make the board available.

We can keep this simple but powerful principle in mind as we look at other items of ELT equipment. And, of course, we'll remember to clean the board before we leave.

Technology

Contemporary ELT has a lot of electrical and electronic equipment to consider, the most common items being the overhead projector, the audiocassette player and the videocassette player. Some teachers will be faced with all these machines at the very beginning of their careers; some teachers will never see any of them in their classrooms. I am going to make some general points about them all, followed by a few detailed comments on each.

First of all, here is one (only half-joking) warning to keep in mind:

> If you are dependent on technology, you may already be halfway into trouble.

Unlike the board, all the above pieces of equipment can go wrong, not to mention the possibility of problems with the electricity supply. So, first of all, make sure that:

- the machinery is where you want it to be;
- it is working;
- the results are visible and/or audible from all parts of the room;
- whatever material you want to use is in place and ready for use;
- you have already seen and/or listened to the material yourself.

If your machine then breaks down, the students will probably be sympathetic, but they will still want teaching. So, be sure you know:

- how to do an elementary check, at least to the extent of: Is it plugged in? Turned on at the mains? Turned on at the machine?
- who can be asked for help. Perhaps one of the students?
- who should be informed so that the equipment can be fixed as soon as possible.
- what you are going to do right now. Your options are:
    - use the same material some other way (e.g: read out a dialogue);
    - go on to another part of the coursebook or teaching programme;
    - have a 'safety-net' lesson ready for use at any time. (I find storytelling useful here.)

More positively, here are some general points about first approaches:

- Don't let unfamiliar equipment put you off. A videocassette player is no more complicated or difficult than an audiocassette player.
- Ask a colleague to show you how something works. Other teachers are often afraid of 'interfering', but are also often happy to help if asked, especially with something they are enthusiastic about.
- Spend some time familiarising yourself with the equipment. Don't underestimate the importance of hands-on experience.
- Experience the equipment from the learner's point of view. Sit in the laboratory, for example, and go through the materials as a student receives them.
- Look out for opportunities to let students work the equipment in class. Having someone else carry out simple mechanical tasks can be quite extraordinary in its effect of turning students into participants.

It is worth remembering that the equipment we are considering here shares one common feature with all language teaching materials. We begin by asking 'How do I use this?' but it is very important to progress to the question 'Why do I use this?' Otherwise, we have students sitting in front of video screens simply because the school has the technology. In this case, what should be an aid to learning has become a high-tech way of passing the time. We shall not go far wrong if we keep on asking ourselves how our use of equipment relates to the underlying issues of communication, feelings, rules, practice, and strategies inside a general context of motivation.

In the brief notes that follow, therefore, I shall concentrate on *why* one would want to use these machines. I shall leave you to follow up the details of *how* to use them if it is useful to do so in your setting. Further readings are listed at the end of the book.

The overhead projector

The overhead projector (OHP) has two very positive characteristics:

- You can prepare a lot of written or visual material before the class.
- You can face the students while writing or pointing things out.

Again, there is no need to be possessive about the OHP. The overhead transparency (OHT) is a very useful way of having a group present notes on work they have done. Or, if one group member has been listening out for mistakes during an activity, these can be written on an OHT for the whole class to discuss.

Some photocopiers can copy onto some OHTs. Be careful. If you melt the wrong kind of OHT inside the school's photocopier, your colleagues may want to do the same thing to you! Normal size print, such as this, is unlikely to be big enough for an OHP. And get someone to show you how to change the bulb before you come to that emergency in class.

The audiocassette player

The audiocassette is useful for bringing a variety of voices and interactions into class. As such, it is often central to the presentation of new language to be learnt (see Chapter 7), and to the provision of listening practice (see Chapter 9). When you bring in outside materials, encourage your students to do the same thing. You may have to listen to some awful songs, but if your students are thinking about recording English, they are more likely to be listening to the English that is available to them.

As well as bringing the outside world into the classroom, the tape recorder can be used to help students concentrate on the English they use in the classroom. One group can be recorded during an activity. This causes awkwardness at first, but people soon get used to it. You can use the recording in a variety of ways, for example:

- Simply let the group members take the cassette home and listen to themselves. Ask each one to tell you one thing they have learnt from listening to the tape.
- While the rest of the class does the next activity, have the group work together on the tape. They should prepare to report back to the class on mistakes they noticed and corrected, and on things they thought they said really well.

The audiocassette player is a part of everyday life for a great many people. People can and do listen to tapes while walking, while driving, and while lying in bed. You simply need to apply your ingenuity to motivating them to listen to English.

The videocassette player

Video provides information to eyes and ears, so students can see communication in action. It also gives us a chance to separate sound and vision in the teaching of language in use. At its simplest, you can show a brief exchange on screen without sound and ask students, 'What are they doing?' 'What are they saying?'

You can sometimes choose your clip to focus initially on particular language functions. In the discussion of what the characters are doing, you can draw attention to typical facial expressions, gestures or body movements. When predicting what people are saying, you can draw attention to the social appropriacy of different ways of expressing the functions. So, if you think that one person has asked another to do something, what would be the most suitable form of request to use? When you do play the sequence with sound, you have provided a very good reason for careful listening.

For variety, you can also reverse this procedure, playing first the sound only and asking students to predict the situation, characters and relationships involved.

Remember that people spend a lot of time watching television, and they are probably used to a reasonably high quality of sound and vision. Poor quality in these areas can be very demotivating. Moreover, people have their television-watching habits, which are probably a long way away from concentrated viewing for learning. Teaching with video has to be distinguished from watching TV. So, keep video extracts short, and make sure that students have something to look out for: a good reason for viewing.

The overall message of this chapter is that the immediate classroom environment can and will exert a powerful influence on the teaching and learning which take place. Make yourself comfortable in your space and with the equipment you intend to use there.

We have now completed our period of familiarisation with the ELT classroom, and we have also noted some principles and procedures which are of use to us when we want to make the elements of that classroom interact. That was the easy part.

Questions and activities

Think about your responses and then discuss them with a colleague.

1 Think about rooms in which you have studied. Do you agree that the room and its furniture had an effect on the work that was done there, or your enjoyment of it?

2 Much of what is said about furniture and interaction has an ideological base: it assumes that giving people freedom and responsibility is a good thing. Is this necessarily the case everywhere? In an authoritarian society, couldn't this cause problems? What problems might it cause? What do you learn from this?

3 What problems might you meet if you follow the suggestion of 'making the board available'? How do you react to this?

4 What experience do you have as a learner or teacher of the equipment written about in this chapter? How do you feel about using it? Note down any problems, questions, or ideas you have and discuss them with a colleague.

5 If there are pieces of equipment which are not available to you, did you notice anything in the chapter which suggests that there are some important things you cannot do without that equipment? If so, write them down and think about ways of achieving the same learning opportunities without the technology.

Part Two
Action

In Part One of the book, we familiarised ourselves with the main elements of any ELT situation and looked at examples of teaching techniques on the way. In Part Two, we concentrate more directly on actual teaching procedures and take the background as read. We look at how to:

- plan and manage classroom activity;
- introduce and practise new language;
- choose appropriate techniques for correction;
- organise learning through communication;
- teach the skills of listening, reading, speaking and writing;
- use tests and teach in the context of formal examinations;
- continue your own personal and professional development in ELT.

In all of these chapters, you will see the importance of the issues we have already discussed. In this way, the book tries to base action on understanding. Your part is to continue to relate the generalities of the book to the specifics of your own experience.

Please remember that the book can offer *ways* of doing these things, but not *the* way of doing them. Every idea can be improved and adapted; there is always another argument. And once you have found out which procedures suit you best, it is a good idea to use others sometimes. Variety of method is both a part of good teaching and a basis for the teacher's own development. And the issue of teacher development is what motivates the final chapter. In this way, the book tries to stay in line with the methodological principle which underlies all the teaching suggestions in it: we begin with the learner and what the learner knows, move with the learner into the unknown, and then focus again on the learner to ask, 'What can you do now?' The overall purpose is to help more learners and teachers decide for themselves what their next steps will be.

 # Managing

In Chapter 5, we talked about how and why we might use the equipment that we have available. In this chapter, we look at ways of managing the events and the people. We shall focus on the *planning, interactions,* and *language* of classroom management. In practice, these issues are not separate from methodology. I have separated them in order to focus on them clearly now, and to concentrate on other matters of teaching method in the chapters which follow.

Planning

In this section, we are going to concentrate on lesson plans, but first we have to take in two aspects of a bigger picture.

Firstly, even if you have no planning responsibilities beyond your own classes, your overall planning needs to extend beyond just the end of the next lesson.

If you are working with published or previously prepared materials, do find the time to read ahead, both through the materials themselves and the teacher's guide. At least skim through the book and read in some detail to the end of the next unit, so that you have an overview of what is coming up. This is not idealistic advice – it is good survival strategy. You can feel very silly if you can't answer today a question which the book gets into tomorrow.

In some teaching situations, forward planning is very difficult. If you find yourself teaching a sequence of unconnected lessons where you deal with whatever turns up, pause after every few lessons to go back over what has been done. Review this with the students and make a record together of what they have learnt. You might use the headings: *words, grammar, functions, pronunciation* and *discourse,* together with any useful *strategies*. In this way, you will give shape to what has been done and connections will emerge. This will certainly also help your students to remember and consolidate new language.

Secondly, it is always worthwhile finding out about your students' backgrounds and motivations. Here are two sample questionnaires which can inform you and raise your learners' awareness about the situations in which they use English, the skills they need, and what is most important for them to work on. This should help you choose supplementary materials to add to what your coursebook offers and help your students to focus their learning efforts.

Needs analysis chart

Situations	Skills					
	Vocabulary (✓)	Grammar (✓)	Listening (✓)	Speaking (✓)	Reading (✓)	Writing (✓)

Record of priorities

Skill	Priority rating
Extending vocabulary	
Dealing with grammar	
Listening	
Speaking	
Reading	
Writing	

Ex. 6.1 (Ellis and Sinclair 1989: 109)

Lesson plans

We shall concentrate on the lesson plan as a practical, working document. If you are studying for a teaching certificate of some kind, you will probably find that your ability to produce a lesson plan is one part of your assessment. In these circumstances, you need to find out exactly what your lesson plans should contain, how they should be laid out, and how they will be assessed. The points made here will underlie any more complicated model which you are asked to produce for examination purposes.

The process of writing a lesson plan should help you clarify your answers to the following questions:

- What are the objectives of this lesson?
- How am I going to achieve these objectives?
- How shall I know if I have achieved my objectives or not?

The lesson plan itself should then act as a reminder during the lesson of your answers to these questions.

Let's look at the questions in more detail and then put a plan together.

What are the objectives of this lesson?

The clearest way of answering this question is to specify objectives in terms of what your students will be able to do at the end of the lesson. So, for example, you might write:

By the end of this lesson, students will be able to name all the items of clothing worn in class.
or:
By the end of this lesson, students will be able to distinguish between /p/ and /b/ at the beginning of words when listening and speaking.
or:
By the end of this lesson, students will be able to use the Present Progressive (with 'probably') to describe what other members of their family are doing while we are here learning English. e.g: 'My brother is probably having lunch.'

It is important to keep thinking about what the students will be able to do, even though it is not always possible to be so exact. If the purpose of a lesson is more vague, such as: 'to give further practice of reading skills', then so be it. But perhaps you can sharpen up your thinking (and your teaching) if you try to be more specific. For example:

By the end of the lesson, students will have gained further practice in:
- skimming to gather an overall impression of a text;
- improving their reading speed by timed reading;
- justifying answers to questions by reference to the text;
- relating the content of the text to their own experience.

How am I going to achieve these objectives?

This is the main body of the plan, where you list the various steps of the lesson in terms of:

- what you are going to do;
- what the students are going to do;
- how long each step is going to take.

Whatever the specific focus of your lesson is, each lesson should feature good human relations. We aren't going to write this on a lesson plan, but that doesn't make it less important. Just exactly what the appropriate relationships are will depend on you, your students and the context in which you work, but do allow time for the greetings and exchanges (about appearance, clothes, sport, television, etc.) which acknowledge each lesson as a social event.

On some occasions, these exchanges may be enough to get the students both settled in and warmed up ready to start work. On other occasions, it is useful to use a short warm-up activity to pull the class together and prepare them to start the lesson proper. These activities can be quick and fun and, once you start to think about it, you'll develop ideas that suit your own way of being a teacher. Here are two examples of my own:

- physical:
  Everyone reach out and touch someone else so that everyone is touching. Now go, 'Mmmmmmmmmmmmmmmmmm.'

- intellectual:
  What's four times two? Plus eight? Times three? Divided by twelve? Plus thirty-seven? Minus eighteen?

Alternatively, a warm-up might be more closely linked to the goals of the lesson, as in the *Anagrams* activity in our lesson plan (p. 68).

As a lesson gets under way, it is frequently a good idea to refer back to a related previous lesson. Recycling earlier material helps students remember and learn it. It also helps them make connections between what they know already and what they are about to learn. If nothing else, it gets the students back into an 'Ah yes, English lessons' frame of mind. Then we get on to the main business of the current lesson.

One clear layout for a plan is four columns: one for the teacher, one for the students, one to show the interactions between the teacher and students, and one for timing. With experience, you will probably develop your own shorthand, but it is a good idea to keep these points separate at first. Whether you write interactions separately or not, it is important that your plan should provide a variety of interaction as the lesson proceeds. There is more about interaction in the next section of this chapter.

The most common weakness of lesson plans is unrealistic timing. A great teacher fear is of 'not having enough material'. This leads to lessons over-full of material, but with no time for any learning to take place. In a normal teaching situation, what doesn't get done this lesson is pushed into the next lesson without any great problem arising. But if this happens on a regular basis, it becomes clear as the weeks pass that students are not going to reach the stage that they were supposed to reach by the end of the term, or course. So, time the steps of your lessons beforehand, and take the trouble to write in the real timings afterwards. As you develop an informed sense of what is likely to be achieved in real time, you are developing a skill that will be invaluable when you become involved in course planning.

How shall I know if I have achieved my objectives or not?

The more exactly you have described your objectives in terms of what the students will be able to do, the easier it is to check them. In terms of the objectives set above, for instance, you could use these procedures at the end of the lesson to see if your teaching was successful:

By the end of this lesson, students will be able to name all the items of clothing worn in class.

Teacher	Students	Interaction	Time
Nominate student	S1 stands, points to an item of his/her clothing and nominates S2. S2 names item and continues procedure.	T→S→S	5 mins.

By the end of this lesson, students will be able to distinguish between /p/ and /b/ at the beginning of words when listening and speaking.

Teacher	Students	Interaction	Time
Put two lists of words on board, saying each one. Words in List 1 start with /p/. Words in List 2 start with /b/.	Ss read and listen.	T→Ss	2 mins.
Say a word from one list.	Ss call out: '1' or '2'.	T↔Ss	2 mins.
Say a word and nominate S.	S says '1' or '2'.	T↔S	2 mins.
Nominate S1.	S1 says a word, then nominates S2. S2 says '1' or '2'.	T→S→S	2 mins.

These timings can only be approximate, but you wouldn't want to spend more than ten minutes on either of these activities, because they would be boring. In a large class, you would nominate a sample of your students to give you an idea of what the class had learnt.

Other issues also arise from these 'examples'. With the first one, there will be a lot more life in the exercise if you have a multi-national mix of young men and women, than if your class is made up only of children in a strict school uniform. The second example assumes that the distinction between /p/ and /b/ is a problem for your students, otherwise the objective was nonsense. In other words, any 'example' of a teaching or checking technique is a poor thing unless it arises in a real context.

Having said that, let's look at some materials written for adults who began their course with little or no English and have progressed to Unit 6 of their coursebook.

My plan sets objectives and starts you off in the lesson. I then invite you to turn to the questions and activities at the end of the chapter (Question 5).

6 *This is your life*

Jobs; *a/an* + jobs; *What do you do?*

Revision

1 Name these jobs.

Example: a tesutdn – a student
a reetach
a aiwtre
a hsop tssasitan

2 🔊 Listen. What is this person's job?

3 Listen again. Which of these things does she do at work?

open the shop   answer the phone
read sports magazines   teach English
write letters   serve customers
cook

Which of these things does she like doing?

Vocabulary: jobs

1 Write three sentences about your job or the job of another person in your family. Do not name the job! Think about these questions.

Where do you work?
What do you do at work?
What do you like doing at work?

2 Read your sentences to other students. They guess the name of your job.

3 Ask other students about their jobs.

Example: A: What do you do?
          B: I'm a teacher

4 Write what you remember. Ask again if necessary. Mark the stress on the jobs.

☐
Maria is a dentist
☐
Julio is a teacher

Pronunciation: *do*

1	2
/dju/	/duː/
What do you do?	

1 🔊 Listen. Which *do* is stressed, 1 or 2?

2 🔊 Listen to these questions. Which word has got main stress?

1 Where do you work/study?
2 What do you do at work/school/university?
3 What time do you start?
4 What time do you finish?

3 Ask another student the questions above.

Reading

1 Before you read, look at the pictures below. Find an astronaut, a politician, a soldier and a pilot.

2 Look at the pictures again. How many famous people can you name?

Ex. 6.2 (Mohamed
        and Acklam
        1992: 34)

Length of class: 1 hour (e.g. 11.00–12.00)

Objectives: By the end of the lesson, students will be able to:
— talk about their own jobs and ask classmates about theirs.
— use the Present Simple accurately and fluently in this context.
— choose correctly between a/an.
— pronounce the unstressed form of 'd'you' /djʊ/ in their questions.

Materials: Mohamed and Acklam 1992: 34, Unit 6.

Teacher	Students	Interaction	Time
1 Show e.g. of Ex. 1.1.	Solve anagrams.	T↔Ss	11.00
Ask for answers to be spelt.	Practise spelling.		
Invite pairs to make up new anagrams. Write these on board.	Make up anagrams.	S↔S pairs	
Elicit answers inc. spelling.	Practise spelling.	T↔Ss	11.05
2 Ask Ss to identify job in 1.2.		T→Ss	
Play tape and check all agree. Replay if necessary.	Listen and respond.	T↔Ss	
3 Elicit probable answers to 1.3 before playing. Point out question about *likes*.	Answer, then listen to check.	T↔Ss	
Play tape and nominate Ss to answer. Check third person singular *-s* endings.	Answer about likes.		11.15

It is highly unlikely that an experienced teacher would write out anything as explicit as my plan, for two good reasons.

Firstly, this plan was written to communicate with someone else, while a practical lesson plan is written only for the use of its writer. Secondly, the more experienced you are, the easier it is to write a short note that will mean a lot to you. But none of this is an argument against writing lesson plans. Students depend on teachers to have a clear sense of purpose and a way of proceeding towards that purpose in real time. Both as a way of preparing yourself to teach, and helping you teach, I know of no substitute for a lesson plan, and it pays to begin with a clear and explicit framework. After twenty years of ELT, it still would not occur to me to go into class without a lesson plan, although I admit it would no longer look like the one I have written here.

On my plan, I have marked the intended teacher ↔ student and student ↔ student interactions. Let us look at this in more detail.

Interactions

When we talk about different interactions in class, we mean the issue of who is speaking to whom. Let us look at some common examples.

The teacher sometimes gives instructions to the whole class (T → Ss) and sometimes to an individual (T → S). Sometimes, there will be an exchange between the teacher and the whole class (T ↔ Ss) and sometimes the teacher will tell one student to say something to another (T → S → S). Sometimes, students will communicate directly with each other (S ↔ S). We also want to see communication with the teacher started by students (S ↔ T), but this is behaviour we can encourage rather than something we can plan.

A movement from interaction between the teacher and the whole class to interaction between students themselves (either in pairs or groups) is the most usual pattern of interaction in modern ELT. Generally the teacher ↔ class interaction aims to promote accuracy; the student ↔ student interaction aims to promote fluency.

> Using language in different interactions is as important to language learning as studying different forms of language.

Other advantages of varied interactions for classroom teaching are:

- a change of interaction brings a change of focus of attention, which helps keep people interested;
- in pairs and groups, there is opportunity for many more individuals to use the language;
- students perform differently away from the pressure of teacher and whole-class attention;
- students learn to be more self-reliant;
- taking the focus of attention away from the teacher gives the teacher a chance to listen and evaluate what has been learnt.

Some teachers worry about their lack of control when they use pairwork or groupwork, but this is to misunderstand the teacher's power and role.

> The teacher is not asked to give up control in order to use pairwork and groupwork. The teacher is asked to exercise control in order to use pairwork and groupwork.

Introducing pairwork or groupwork to a situation where it has not been used before is difficult for two main reasons:

- conflict with the students' ideas of what 'being taught' means;
- conflict with colleagues' ideas of what 'being a teacher' means.

These are not arguments against introducing pairwork and groupwork; they are grounds for proceeding slowly and carefully. Here are some suggestions:

1 Explain the purpose of pairwork and groupwork, as outlined above. Use the students' first language if it helps.

2 Begin with pairwork under direct supervision. One way to start is to have students do an exercise individually and then check it with their neighbour. This could be done with Exercise 1.1 on page 67.

The S↔S pairwork in Exercise 2.2 can also be done by two students sitting next to each other. To begin with, the teacher tells the students very explicitly which twos are working together, and then says:
Everyone on this side of the pair is Student A. Everyone on the other side is Student B.
Student A, read out your three sentences quietly now to Student B.
OK, Student B, guess the name of the job now.
Right, all you A students, if your Student B guessed the job correctly, raise your hands.
Student B, if you didn't guess correctly, try again now.

After a while, this amount of control can be reduced to:
Please do this exercise in pairs.

3 As students become more used to pairwork, you can move on to a freer approach. Let us take the simple example of practising *How many* with plural nouns. You can compile a list of nouns to suit your students: with children it might be *brothers and sisters*; with adults it might be *children*; it is the teacher's business to work this out in context with the learners.

Students make a simple questionnaire by writing the names of five or ten classmates on a piece of paper. They then go to those people and collect the information.

How many _____ do you have?

Name	children	sons	daughters
Pedro	3	1	2
Clara	0	–	–
Ahmed	1	1	0
Yoko			

If the students were encouraged to write the names of people they did not know very well, think what effect this simple exercise could have in terms of meaningful practice, real communication, and feelings about the relationships in the class.

4 So far, we have spoken about groupwork as though it were the same as pairwork, because it is S↔S interaction. In one important way, however, it is not. In pairwork, when one person is silent, the other person is usually called on to speak. In groupwork, it is possible for a person to remain silent and let others carry out the task. Now, as we know, some people talk more than others, and people learn differently, so we need not rush to define different amounts of talk as a problem. Nevertheless, we have to guard against the possibility that a group member would like to speak, but is not getting the chance. There are two ways you can respond to this situation:

● In terms of the task itself, make sure that each person has something to contribute to the whole. Notice in the task below how students are first invited to prepare an individual contribution and then to share that with a partner. They then move into group discussion, where the need for communication arises out of their individual differences:

Write down what you eat and drink at mealtimes and for snacks in a typical day. Then interview a partner and add details of his/her eating habits.

Work with another pair and give details about yourself and your partner. Say:

a) how much meat or fish you eat on a typical day.
b) how many sweet things you eat.
c) how much you drink.
d) what you eat a lot of.
e) what you eat a little of.
f) whether you think you have a healthy diet. (Give reasons.)

Look at the *Checklist for Healthy Eating* and the examples below. Discuss in groups. What do you think you eat too much of? What do you think you don't eat enough of? Example:

Paul eats chocolate all the time. He eats too much chocolate.
He hardly ever eats any fruit. He doesn't eat enough fruit.
He eats chips everyday. He eats too many chips.

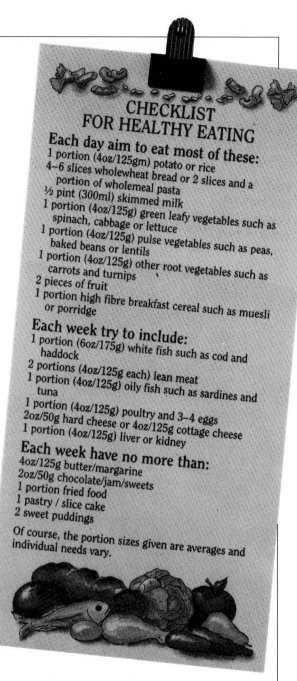

CHECKLIST FOR HEALTHY EATING

Each day aim to eat most of these:
1 portion (4oz/125gm) potato or rice
4–6 slices wholewheat bread or 2 slices and a portion of wholemeal pasta
½ pint (300ml) skimmed milk
1 portion (4oz/125g) green leafy vegetables such as spinach, cabbage or lettuce
1 portion (4oz/125g) pulse vegetables such as peas, baked beans or lentils
1 portion (4oz/125g) other root vegetables such as carrots and turnips
2 pieces of fruit
1 portion high fibre breakfast cereal such as muesli or porridge

Each week try to include:
1 portion (6oz/175g) white fish such as cod and haddock
2 portions (4oz/125g each) lean meat
1 portion (4oz/125g) oily fish such as sardines and tuna
1 portion (4oz/125g) poultry and 3–4 eggs
2oz/50g hard cheese or 4oz/125g cottage cheese
1 portion (4oz/125g) liver or kidney

Each week have no more than:
4oz/125g butter/margarine
2oz/50g chocolate/jam/sweets
1 portion fried food
1 pastry / slice cake
2 sweet puddings

Of course, the portion sizes given are averages and individual needs vary.

Ex. 6.3 (Bell and Gower 1991: 107)

- As students become accustomed to groupwork, encourage them to pay attention to how they interact in groups. Tell them:
  If you find that you are talking a lot, or that someone else is not saying much, then ask that person, 'What do you think?'

5 The more freedom you give your students, the more important it is that they understand exactly what they are supposed to do. So, before the pairwork or groupwork starts:
  - ask one of the students to repeat the instructions, or
  - have one pair or one group demonstrate the activity to the class.

6 During pairwork and groupwork, you need to be available to help where necessary, but the main part of your job is to move round and listen in order to be able to evaluate progress and eventually give feedback (see Chapter 7).

7 Physically speaking, four or five is an ideal size for a group. Six people will probably split up into two sub-groups. Also, students need to be actually *in* a group; a line of students is *not* a group.

8 Tasks for pairwork and groupwork should:
  - be clearly understood in English;
  - include input in and work with English (note how students in Ex. 6.3 opposite have to refer to the Checklist);
  - involve some spoken or written outcome in English. (Ex. 6.3 leads the students into a role-play in which they argue for different kinds of diet. See Chapter 8.)

As long as these criteria are met, we shall not get too upset if we sometimes hear the students using their first language.

This last point deserves some discussion in its own right, because we have repeatedly argued for the importance of using English as the language of the classroom, both for teaching and for management purposes.

First language and second language

In classrooms where learners come from different language backgrounds, the teacher has no choice but to communicate somehow in English. In this situation, I have found that even if I do speak the language of some of the students, I prefer not to use this ability, as it threatens the unity of the class.

In classrooms where all learners share a language, we call this language their L1. In ELT, the L2 is English.

Wherever possible, run your class in English. That means all the social business of saying good morning, taking the register, handing out papers, and everything else that happens in class. If all this is done in English:

- it demonstrates very clearly that English is a form of living communication to be used, not just a subject to be studied;
- it gives students extra practice in hearing and using English;
- it gives students a chance to acquire some language naturally;
- it introduces forms and uses of the language which the syllabus will not cover.

So, speak simply and clearly, support what you say with gestures and actions, but insist on running the class in English. You may meet resistance and/or giggles, but it is worth persevering.

> If you can involve your students in this small, English-using community, you have made one of your most important contributions to their learning.

Two warnings:

- Don't insist on the use of English if the level of frustration on a particular occasion becomes negative. If the students really cannot understand you, or if a student really cannot express something that he or she clearly very much wants to say, then use the L1. Then make a point of showing the class how this is said in English – they will be just ready to learn it. If you don't speak the L1, let the whole class work on helping you.
- Don't become depressed if students continue to use their L1 among themselves. In a monolingual class, it takes a great amount of dedication to struggle with an L2 when you can say what you want to so easily in your L1. Some teachers use praise, some use threats, some use fines in order to stop the use of L1. The important thing is that students know why you go on making such a fuss about the use of English, and that the atmosphere remains good-humoured.

Before finishing this section, we can extend a little further the idea of a classroom community. Make every effort to encourage small, everyday exchanges between people in English:

Teacher: Ahmed, you look very tired today!
Ahmed: Yes, I very tired. Last night go disco.
Teacher: Ah, did you have a good time?
Ahmed: Yes, very good, but come home three o'clock.

Teacher: You came home at three! Well, try to stay awake now and you
           can have a nap *(mime)* for ten minutes between lessons!

You then need to keep a balance between the desires of different
learners to communicate and to be correct:

Yoshiko: Ahmed should say, he *went* to the disco, I think so.
Teacher: That would be grammatically correct, Yoshiko, but I understood
           very well what Ahmed was saying to me. Did you do anything
           interesting last night?

Finally, with regard to the classroom community, we have to say
something about possible problems of unacceptable behaviour. First
of all, if you do not share the cultural and linguistic background of
your students, try to inform yourself of the kind of behaviour they
expect in class. Even if you do share that background, remember that
if you are introducing new forms of activity, it will not always be clear
to students exactly what the rules are or where the changes end.

Questions of conduct are so tied to particular societies that I will
treat this subject only from a language teaching angle. Wherever
possible, make classroom behaviour a topic of discussion. At
elementary level, you can work at building up a code of conduct in
simple English, for example:
Students always do their homework on time.
The teacher always returns the homework next lesson.   or:
If students come to class late, . . .
If the teacher comes to class late, . . .

With more advanced students, you might start a discussion with:

What kind of	teacher / student	behaviour is most	helpful / harmful	to learning?

Building a community with shared rules will not solve all discipline
problems, but if you make behaviour an open topic, you can help
prevent problems arising. And if you are consistent in your behaviour
and your classes are clearly well-prepared, you can expect the
support of your English-using community when difficulties do occur.

The keys to management are **communication, choice** *and*
commitment*. Fortunately, they are also the keys to
language learning. Work with your students to plan
relevant objectives in a realistic timescale.*

Questions and activities

Think about your responses and then discuss them with a colleague.

1   Have you ever used a questionnaire to find out about your students' needs? Was it useful?

2   Has any teacher ever used a questionnaire with you as a student? Was it useful? How would you respond to the questionnaires on page 62 in terms of a language you would like to learn?

3   In your experience as a learner or teacher, how easy is it to describe objectives in terms of what students will be able to do?

4   Look through some materials, if possible with a specific group of students in mind. How many lessons would you expect to spend on those materials? Alternatively, how much material would you need for a one-hour class? Compare your responses with those of a colleague.

5   Complete a one-hour lesson plan to achieve and check the objectives given on page 68.

6   Can you suggest general improvements to the style of my lesson plan? How could you personalise it for your own use? If you are studying for a teaching certificate, how does this plan compare to what is required of you?

7   What interactions did you experience in class as a learner? Which do you use as a teacher? How do individual styles or cultural background affect this?

8   What dangers do you see in treating the class as a 'social event', as well as a formal lesson? What do you learn from your response?

9   What experience do you have of discipline problems, either as a student or teacher? How do you think they should be treated?

Methodology 1: From language to communication

> The only serious answer to the question, 'How do you teach English?' is, 'It depends.'

Because that answer is true but unhelpful, we are going to consider others which are less true but more useful. We have already talked about the importance of creating a safe, English-using environment in which students feel encouraged to express themselves. In that environment, here is one simplified outline of an approach to language teaching:

1 You introduce meaningful models of language the students need.

2 You conduct careful practice of the language.

3 You organise communicative interaction.

4 You give feedback on the students' use of the language.

We can see a commonsense sequence here: students learn something new, practise it, use it meaningfully and find out from the teacher how they are getting on. We also saw this sequence in Chapter 4, when we talked about a possible move from published materials to local materials. But do note that these are not fixed stages of a lesson. This is not even a simple sequence of events. It is a list of points which are all bound up with each other. As in Chapter 2, we shall unpick the strands in order to be able to talk about them separately.

As we discuss the above points, I shall exemplify them from teaching materials, beginning with the materials we used in the lesson plan in Chapter 6. Please refer back to those materials during the chapter.

There is a teaching decision involved here. I could have used different examples from different books. This would have made us familiar with a wider range of materials. I am reusing one extract in the hope of showing more clearly how lesson plans, materials and methods hang together.

> This kind of decision is central to methodology: you decide to do one thing rather than another; you gain something and you lose something.

One final point: please remember that I am *not* suggesting that we teach English by following a coursebook. We are using sample materials to help us imagine teaching procedures. We use the procedures to help us talk about underlying principles. Your task is then to relate these principles to procedures and materials which are appropriate in your own situation.

Introducing meaningful models of language

It is easy, but mistaken, to think of the introduction of new language as the beginning of a lesson. The teaching procedure should begin before that introduction if the learning is going to be successful. We have already mentioned the importance of:

- a warm-up period to get the class under way;
- a review of something learnt earlier which is particularly relevant to what is coming. (Introducing something new in the context of something known should be a regular feature of teaching.)

Furthermore, as well as being sure about the relevance of the language to the students as learners, we have to be sure that it is relevant to them as people. These issues are clearly not separate. Let's return to *This is Your Life* (page 67).

We know from our lesson plan (and the students know from the box of items at the beginning of the unit) what our immediate objectives are. We can answer our questions about the relevance of the new language as follows:

- It is relevant to the students as learners because it is a logical next step in helping them master the rules of verb tense formation and become aware of how tenses refer to time.
- It is relevant to the students as people, because it will enable a group of individuals who probably do not know each other very well to communicate appropriately with each other and about each other. This will give them authentic social practice and improve the feeling among the group.

So, let's get into the lesson at a time after the local greetings and warm-up have taken place:

1.1 sets a simple task which reminds students of some job
names met earlier. It also prepares them for 1.2, where
the answer will be *shop assistant*.

1.2 sets a simple task for a first listening to someone talking
about her job. Tell the students what they are listening
for and play the tape. Ask for an answer. Don't indicate
whether or not the first answer is correct, ask others if
they agree or disagree. If there is disagreement, or you
feel that many students are not sure, play the tape again.
The process of listening and making up their minds is
more useful to the students than simply getting a right
answer to an exercise.

1.3 sets a more difficult task for the second listening. Tell
students to read the exercise and check vocabulary before
they listen again. As well as reviewing vocabulary, this
exercise reviews the use of the Present Simple to describe
habitual action. As the students give their responses, they
will be practising adding the third person -*s*: 'She opens
the shop.' The exercise also reviews *like doing*, a form of
expression which the students learnt earlier.

So, topics, vocabulary, structures and functions from earlier lessons
have been reactivated. In this instance, the published materials have
taken care of this stage of the teaching. On other occasions, you will
have to take more responsibility for this yourself.

New language can be provided by the teacher or by the materials, or
it can be elicited from the students. This last possibility is worth
exploring in its own right.

Elicitation

> Before you 'teach' something, find out if your students
> already know it.

So, if the next lesson teaches how to make a request, you can begin
by miming not having a pen to write something with, or wanting a
window open, or needing a dictionary, and ask your class, 'What do I
say?' If you only get suggestions such as, 'Give pen!' you can tell that
you need to present the new language carefully. If you get lots of
suggestions such as, 'Would you mind opening the window for me,
please?' you have been warned against spending a lot of time on
presentation; you can take the lesson at a brisk pace and draw
language models from the students.

Your learners will probably be somewhere in between those two extremes. The point is that you need to know where they are. Encourage them to show you what they know, or think they know. Make it clear that you will accept their attempts without correction at this stage. This helps you see where your teaching can usefully begin. Afterwards, students can check what they have learnt against what they thought before.

> Learning and teaching begin out on the edge of what the students already know.

Another important use of elicitation is when a student asks a question and you turn this question back to the class:

Student: Do we say, 'When they had *sat* down', or 'When they had *sut* down'?

Teacher: Would anyone like to answer that?/Let's see what other people think.

You need to be careful here not to hurt anyone's feelings. Explain that the idea is:

- to show that students can learn from each other;
- to encourage a feeling of working together;
- to take the threat out of being corrected by a colleague.

If you can encourage this atmosphere, you have gone a long way towards enabling students to work and learn in groups without your constant presence.

Presentation

We want to present new language items meaningfully, in some kind of communicative context, in a way which will make their use clear. This is one reason why you will often find new grammatical structures first shown in a dialogue. Another reason is that, by practising a dialogue in pairs, students can be involved in an appearance of interaction. They may thus get a feel for how the language is used, as well as an understanding of how the new grammar works.

Remember also how in Ex. 4.2 (Chapter 4), we talked about the students understanding a tape functionally before focusing on the language used. Here again, the idea of communication is already present at the beginning of the procedure.

Let us look at what happens in the *This is Your Life* materials:

2.1 elicits personal information from the students. It gives further practice of the Present Simple for habitual actions, this time in written form. It also reintroduces familiar question forms. If you do the exercise in class, you can circulate and help by providing new vocabulary.

2.2 uses the written preparation of 2.1 to provide support for spoken practice, using new and personal vocabulary in familiar structures.

2.3 introduces the target structure, function, and social exchange. You can easily link this to the previous exercise about the name of your job, by asking: 'When you meet someone and you want to know the name of their job, how do you ask?'
An example of how to ask is clearly given in the book. Notice how unusual the exchange might sound to a beginner: you ask someone what they *do*, and they tell you what they *are*! At this point, the teacher should check that all the students understand that both these expressions refer to someone's *work* or *job*.

So, a new item has been meaningfully introduced and clarified. In this instance, we have followed the procedure of presentation and explanation with reference to materials in a coursebook. It should be clear, however, that it is the principles behind the procedure which are important. It is the teacher's responsibility to make sure that new words, structures and functions are meaningfully presented and properly understood by students. Sometimes, this will involve explicit explanation, to which we now turn.

Explanation

It is impossible to predict in advance exactly which parts of a presentation will not be clear to which students. We do know, however, that some learners need to understand new information (especially grammar) explicitly and appreciate rules of some kind. There are two demands on the teacher:

- that you continue to improve your own understanding of the language systems (words, grammar, functions, discourse, pronunciation) that you are teaching;
- that you use your increasing knowledge to make your explanations shorter, simpler and more relevant.

For example, a student looking at 2.3 above might say:
Sometimes, I think, we say, 'What *are* you do for a living?', no?

The teacher has a variety of possible responses, let's look at some:
1 No.
2 No. Why not?
3 No, to make a question with the Present Simple, we always use the auxiliary, *do.*
4 I like the 'for a living', we do say that, but it's always 'What do you do for a living?', not *are.*
5 No, to ask about things that we do every day like our jobs, we always use *do.*

You might like to think about your own reactions to those responses before you read my comments.

1 This sounds terrible but, in fact, it depends. Some teachers encourage their students to ask as many questions as they like, and they explain to the students that they will always give the shortest answer they can. If that answer is enough, fine. If it is not, ask another question. Perhaps this student can now put this possibility out of mind and get on with learning the correct form. No one else in the class had this problem, so no one's time is wasted. Notice how this technique depends on teacher and students sharing an understanding of how they work together. It is the most extreme response to a danger that all teachers must keep in mind: we sometimes go on and on explaining things because we know them, not because our students need to know them.

2 The teacher's question can be addressed to the individual student or to the whole class. Here, the teacher has decided that some kind of explanation would be helpful. By eliciting it, the teacher hopes to check the class's general understanding of the rule. Basing these exchanges as much as you can on the words that students choose to use helps you establish common terms for talking about language.

3 The teacher believes that the class understands the grammatical terminology necessary for a brief statement of the rule and that for this student, in this situation, it is more efficient for the teacher to state it. Notice how little information the teacher derives from this exchange.

4 The teacher welcomes and repeats the new expression which fits beautifully into the lesson. Notice that the teacher then repeats the correct form, not the incorrect one. The teacher also takes care not to give a false impression of the stress in the sentence

by saying, ' . . . it's always "What *do* you do for a living?", not *are*.' Otherwise, this might have confused students when moving on to the pronunciation exercises. There is no grammatical explanation. Perhaps the teacher wants simply to re-affirm the use of *do* in questions and contrast this with *are* later when the Present Continuous is introduced.

5 The teacher has decided that the student should be reminded of the common function of the form that is being practised here. Establishing this simple link will be most useful for the learner.

To recap, you need to build up with each class an agreed way of talking about English and of asking and answering questions about what is being learnt. Some students will have a background of linguistic terminology and some will not. Sometimes it may be necessary to use the students' first language to explain a grammatical point clearly.

For most learners, security is based on an understanding of how new structures work and how they are used. Based on this understanding, students can go on to develop their own skills in using the language.

Conducting careful practice of the language

The purpose of practice is to help students develop what they know about the language into an ability to use the language. Good practice will provide secure guidance for the learners, but will also do some of the following:

- focus on the students' own lives and experiences (see Chapter 1);
- encourage interaction between students (see Chapter 6);
- practise different language skills of speaking, listening, reading and writing (see Chapter 9) in relation to new items;
- integrate the skills (Chapter 9) by using a listening or reading passage to provide information for practice activities and/or to work as a model for a speaking or writing exercise.

In the last section, we left the lesson at a point where practice of familiar language had been used to introduce the new. Let us return to those materials and look at this practice in more detail.

2.1 suggests individual written practice, drawing on an earlier listening task. This writing should consolidate earlier learning. It also prepares a script for students who might be unsure about speaking in the next exercise. Before the writing, you could nominate students to give you some sample sentences just to make sure that everyone knows what to do.

2.2 You could first read three sentences of your own to the class in order to clarify the task. The student ↔ student practice could then be done in a variety of ways:
- individual student to whole class;
- in pairs;
- in small groups;
- while walking round the room.

At this point, the new language is introduced and requires some initial, supported practice.

2.3 The teacher can begin with some examples addressed to individual students, then move to student ↔ student question and answer with the whole class listening. Whether you yourself nominate both these students, or the first student nominates the second, make sure that the two of them are sitting reasonably far apart: this makes the rest of the class feel included in the exchange, and so provides a clearer example. The practice can then be done in pairs, in groups, or by students walking round the room.

2.4 Here we have written practice again, based on real information, which aims at consolidating individual learning. Pronunciation work is integrated into the practice by making students concentrate on word stress.

In many cases, the practice stage will last longer than here, as students work to make their understanding available for use. We have seen examples of such practice activities in Exs. 2.2 (p. 23) and 4.1 (p. 45).

Here, the grammar of the new item introduced is already familiar and the expression has an immediately interactive function. This means that the class has been able to proceed directly to communicative use. Let us look again at how this happens.

Organising communicative interaction

We have already discussed the importance of communication in ELT (Chapter 2). The main point of relevance here is that we need to provide in the ELT classroom opportunities for the communicative use of the language that is being learnt and practised. Let us look once more at *This is Your Life*:

2.2 already involves communicative interaction. The speaker has true, personal and unpredictable information to communicate and the listeners have a specific task.

2.3 presents a new structural and functional usage which is also used as the basis for careful practice, and which then enables the students to take part in real communication. The power of this little exercise arises from the fact that students are asking for and giving real information about themselves. The teacher has control of structure and function, the students have complete freedom of content.

2.4 is based on what the students can remember about their classmates. This suggests an enjoyable follow-up activity where students read out their sentences to have them checked not just for linguistic correctness, but for factual truth:

Teacher: Right, José, give us a sentence about someone in the class.
José: Sami is a dentist.
Teacher: Who thinks that's true? Please raise your hands. OK, who thinks it's not? Right. Who doesn't know? OK, Sami, is it true?
Sami: Yes, it's true. I'm a dentist. (*Or*, No! It's not true! I'm a cook!)

And all the time, these exchanges are operating to strengthen the relationships among the people in the group.

At this point, I want to move away from the *This is Your Life* materials, as any one set of materials can exemplify only so much. Before we do so, however, let me invite you to look at Steps 1, 2 and 3 under the heading *Pronunciation*, and consider for yourself to what extent the pattern of introducing a model, conducting practice and organising communication is present here.

On other occasions, we also need to organise communication in a looser way, where we provide a context for the use of language, but we do not directly tell the students what to say.

We can see this in the following activity:

Interaction

A friend (A) asked B to take care of his/her house while he/she went away for a few days. But some disasters have happened:

- On Monday B put a box of floppy disks too near the heater. None of the disks will work now.
- On Tuesday B went out and left the house open. Somebody came in and stole the video player and the stereo.
- On Wednesday B used too much detergent in the washing machine, and the machine overflowed. The rug is ruined.
- On Thursday B knocked a cup of coffee over on the television. The television blew up.

It is now Friday. The telephone rings. B picks it up. It is A.
Have the conversation between A and B in which B tells A about all the disasters.

Ex. 7.1 (Harmer and Surguine 1988: 92)

This activity follows a unit which has introduced and practised the following:

- grammar: *must/might/could/should (not) have done something;*
- functions: *speculating about the past; recriminations; apologies.*

Look again at the communicative needs of a foreign language learner (p. 18), and notice how the students' backgrounds and imaginations are being involved here. Different ideas will produce different exchanges. We can see how students could use the recently taught language items, but they are not instructed to. There is a paradox here at the heart of an approach to language teaching which emphasises the importance of communication. In communication, speakers choose freely the forms they use. With free choice of forms, students may not use what we think they should learn.

> Successful learners are likely to be those who consciously take the opportunity to use new language forms in the freer, communicative activities which are offered.

The teacher's job includes making sure that learners see the connections between practice exercises and communicative activities. We have already suggested having a pair or group model an activity before the whole class starts to make sure that everyone understands exactly what to do. This is also a good stage for making sure that students are aware of the linguistic opportunities in front of them.

During a communicative activity, the teacher's main tasks are:

- to make sure as quickly as possible that everyone has understood what they are supposed to be doing, and that they are doing it;
- to be available in case of problems;
- to move round the class and listen carefully so as to be informed about the language the students are using;
- not to interfere.

This last task is often very difficult. Some teachers find it very nearly impossible not to be the centre of attention; some feel that they are not doing their job unless they are correcting, suggesting, explaining, or somehow demonstrating their presence. But there is plenty of work for the teacher to do in the first three tasks mentioned above, even if this work does not look like traditional teaching.

> At some stage, if the learners are to have space to learn, the teacher has to get out of the way.

This is how we try to turn language practice into language use. The more advanced the students, and the more able they are to behave responsibly, the more complex the activities can become. We shall look at examples of such activities in Chapter 8. Here, we have already seen the basic principles beginning to operate from elementary level pairwork and groupwork.

Giving feedback on students' use of language

I made the point at the beginning of the chapter that the four headings I am using are not a series of separate steps in a sequence. The teacher is constantly giving feedback to the students about their use of English. In the *This is Your Life* materials, for example:

1.3 A student might give an answer which is factually accurate, but linguistically incorrect, e.g: 'She open the shop.' As well as a listening task, this is an exercise for careful practice of a recently learnt structure. So, the teacher will want to acknowledge the successful listening, but correct the omission of the third person singular -s. The teacher might say: 'Yes, good, she o . . . ?'

2.1 The teacher moves round the class to check on the accuracy of what is written. This makes sure that students will have a correct script to work from. The teacher might underline a mistake for one student, or write in the correct form for another.

Let us look more closely at the techniques the teacher is using here.

In the introduction to Part Two, I promised advice on correction. Since then, I have been writing about giving feedback. This has been a deliberate attempt to encourage you to give some careful thought to the purposes of correction.

The most common meaning of correction involves pointing out to students in one way or another how close their attempt at English is to some form of standard English. This is important information, and giving this kind of feedback on performance is an important part of teaching. But sometimes, giving this type of feedback can discourage learning.

> This means you have to be sensitive to when a mistake is made and to what kind of a mistake it is, before deciding whether to correct, when to correct, or how to correct.

These distinctions are very important. If a student says, 'Pavarotti is the singer I like him best' the important question for the teacher is not simply whether this is standard English or not. The question is what kind of response from the teacher will be most helpful for the student's continuing learning? Let us look at three possible situations which lead to different answers.

1 During a *controlled exercise* or *drill* to practise relative clauses: the focus is on accuracy and the teacher will want to give immediate feedback. A useful approach is:
   ● Give a chance for self-correction. The teacher might:
      – pull a face to show that there was a mistake, or
      – repeat the sentence up to the mistake and stop: 'Pavarotti is the singer I . . . like . . . ?' to show where the mistake is, or
      – repeat the mistake in such a way as to highlight it: 'him??'

- Move from self-correction, if unsuccessful, to peer correction.
  - Ask if anyone else in the class can help. If they can, go back to the original student for a correct version.

  This technique is useful for:
  - holding class attention;
  - informing the teacher about the class's general level;
  - encouraging the idea that students can learn from each other.

  The technique must be explained, however, and introduced sensitively, or it might hurt people's feelings. This is the point we noted earlier about eliciting answers to student questions.
- Give the standard form yourself as a last resort. If it comes to this, you know that no one in your class was capable of producing the standard form, so the first student did not really make a mistake in something that had been learnt. That student was attempting to say something that your students are not yet able to structure. The idea of correction is therefore not really appropriate – what is needed is more teaching.

2 If you heard this mistake during a *group activity* designed to give an opportunity for communicative use of the language, the focus is on fluency and you wouldn't want to correct immediately. Three useful techniques are:
   - Collect such mistakes as you walk round the class and later put them on the board for discussion without saying who made them.
   - Write the sentence on a slip of paper and later give it to the student as something to think about, perhaps ask about, and learn from.
   - Assign to one group member the task of listening for possible mistakes and raising them for discussion at the end of the task.

3 During an *informal exchange* before, during or after the lesson. The focus is on normal, human conversation in the English-using community which the teacher and students share. In conversation, we very rarely focus on the form of how people say things, we just respond to what they say. What might be appropriate here is to respond naturally and perhaps slip the correct form in without comment later. So, I might well say, 'Yes, he has a wonderful voice. Joni Mitchell is the singer I like best.'

There is one final point to make here about mistakes and correction. We said in Chapter 2 that most learners seem to acquire the forms of a language in a very similar sequence, and this includes the sequence of non-standard forms which students produce while they are learning. The statement 'Pavarotti is the singer I like him best' is certainly unlike standard English. But in the mind of the learner, making this mistake may be a necessary step in learning the standard form.

> Teachers need to encourage students to communicate in the shared knowledge that this must include making mistakes if the language is to develop.

The approach outlined above aims to give appropriate feedback at the appropriate time, so as to encourage language development, while also helping students learn from their mistakes.

Correction is a subject which arouses strong emotions in students and teachers, and is always worth making a topic of discussion both in class and in the staff room. In the meantime, please use at least the first question below to help you review and reflect on this and other points raised in the chapter.

Questions and activities

Think about your responses and then discuss them with a colleague.

1 Look at the four points listed on the first page of this chapter. Think about what each point means to you now. How do these four points relate to the two overall approaches to ELT described in Chapter 2?

2 Look at the materials reproduced in this chapter and relate them to the ideas on communication, feelings, rules, practice and strategy that you read about in Chapter 2.

3 Look at the teaching suggestions in this chapter and relate the teacher's actions to the 'things to be taken care of' in Chapter 1.

4 At every point, the teacher could do something else. For example, with 1.3 of *This is Your Life*, the teacher could simply accept answers from individuals, or carry out a choral drill of the correct answers, or have students write their answers. What would you expect to gain and lose from these different actions? Go through other suggestions. What could you do differently? Why?

5 As a student, how did you feel about being corrected? As a teacher, what do you learn from this?

Methodology 2:
From communication
to language

In the *Questions and activities* section of the last chapter, the second item asked you to look back at Chapter 2, where I suggested that there are two broad approaches to language teaching. If you didn't do so then, let me invite you to do so now.

Communicative activities are a part of both of the approaches outlined in Chapter 2. If you start by presenting separate language items, you will want to progress to the use of those items in some genuine communication. As students attempt to communicate, you will discover whether or not any more formal teaching is necessary. This is what we looked at towards the end of the last chapter.

Sometimes, however, you might want to teach more directly through communicative activities. Perhaps your students have had a lot of previous teaching of separate items which they learnt after a fashion but never got to use. Perhaps they are motivated by having problems to solve in English. Perhaps you have come to believe that people learn a language best through an effort to communicate in it. During such activities, the teacher can monitor progress in order to see to what extent the students might benefit from explicit teaching in some area of language. If you find that there is a general weakness in, for instance, the formation of questions about the future, or a lack of politeness in giving instructions, you might decide to provide some more formal practice in these areas.

So, the two approaches support each other in a continuing fashion: you can enter the cycle at any point. As a rough guide, we can say that the more advanced the students, the more likely they are to want to enter the cycle through a communicative activity.

This process should not, of course, be seen as a circle; it is meant to be a spiral of increasing ability.

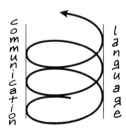

So, let us look more closely at what we mean by the term *communicative activity*. We can think of a communicative activity as a piece of work which involves students in using language in order to get something done. An overall framework for communicative activities would be that students are called upon to:

- *gather* information in English,
- *exchange* information in English, and work together in order to
- *produce* information in English.

We can make activities simpler by taking out one of these stages.

Inside this very general framework, many possible types of activity occur. We are going to look at this broad area from some useful perspectives: tasks, projects, role-plays, simulations and games. We shall not try to describe these as though they were totally separate from each other. It is easy to imagine a project which includes separate tasks, or a role-play inside a game. Also, the terms 'role-play' and 'simulation' are often used interchangeably. Our purpose here is not to draw up definitions, but to answer the same questions which run throughout this book:

- What do people do in modern ELT?
- Why do they do these things?
- How could you do them if you wanted to?

Most of the materials shown in this chapter are for small-scale activities. If you find them interesting, check the references at the end of the book.

Tasks

This is the most general term of the ones we are looking at, meaning sometimes no more than 'something to do'. But even this general meaning is useful to us: tasks are our way of having students do things in English.

Can our students understand a taped dialogue? We could ask them a lot of questions, or we could set them a task:

For Ex. 8.1 opposite, a simple procedure would be:

- *Tell students to look at the picture and ask if there are any questions about vocabulary.* If some are raised, see if other students can supply the words before you do so yourself. If no questions are asked, assume that students are too embarrassed to ask. Tell them to check unknown items with the person next to them. After this, students are more likely to ask openly for words they don't know.
- *Play the tape and have students make notes or mark the picture where they hear differences.* The fact that the students are being

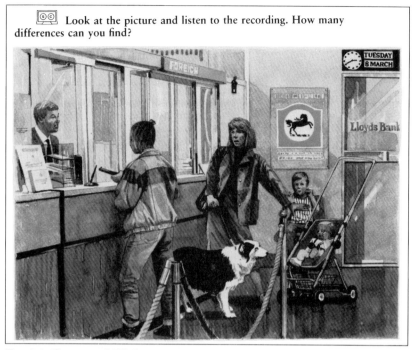

Look at the picture and listen to the recording. How many differences can you find?

Ex. 8.1 (Swan and Walter 1990: 80)

called upon to listen and *do* something is probably already motivating. Notice that their linguistic task in the first place is to *gather* information. At this level the task remains simple.

- *Tell students to check their results in pairs.* Having gathered information, the students *exchange* information with their partners. Although they have listened to the same tape, there may be differences of opinion about what was understood; this is the basis of their exchange.
- *Ask pairs to volunteer their results.* Do not indicate whether you agree or not until all students have agreed, or disagreed and put forward their reasons. Students thus have to *produce* information in the form of a statement of what they see and what they hear. When you have gathered all the responses, play the tape again to clear up disagreements.

As we noted in Chapter 6, we have to accept that some of the information exchange may take place in languages other than English. If this does happen, despite our best efforts at persuasion, we will still know that we are getting information input and output in English. Also, as students know that they will have to give their responses in English, we can encourage them to use some of the information exchange time to prepare that English.

There is one more point to note here before we move on. We talked about the first part of the task being simple. That is to say:

> We can distinguish between difficulty of language and difficulty of task.

This is important because we can balance the two. This, in turn, means that we can motivate learners at elementary level by giving them authentic materials to work with (see Chapter 4), as long as we set them simple tasks to do.

A common type of task in ELT is one in which students are given different information which they must put together. These are called *information gap* activities. Here is an example at intermediate level:

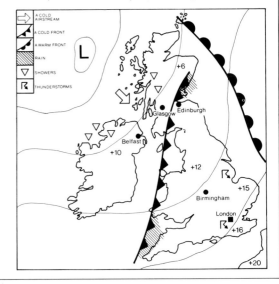

Complete the drawing

Below is an incomplete weather map of Great Britain. Student B has a completed version. He/she is going to help you complete yours.
   You are allowed to ask questions but you must not look at Student B's map.
   When you have finished, compare your drawings.

Complete the drawing

Student A has an incomplete drawing of the weather map of Great Britain.
   Help him/her complete it by telling him/her what to draw and answering his/her questions. But you must not touch his/her map or let him/her see yours.
   When you have finished, compare your drawings.

Ex. 8.2 (Watcyn-Jones 1981: 28)

By giving different information to three or four people who will work in a group, we take this process further. This is often referred to as *jigsaw* listening or reading, because of the need to fit the various pieces together.

As tasks develop in this way, the idea of a linguistic focus becomes more and more difficult to apply, and the idea of a teacher correcting the language of the students as they are involved in the task becomes more and more disruptive.

> If we have asked students to communicate in order to complete a task, then we should let them get on with it.

We looked in Chapter 7 at how you can give feedback after a task.

Projects

We have seen how tasks can become more and more complicated in terms of what students are asked to do as they gather, exchange and produce information. All the information in the above examples was provided in the materials themselves. We can, however, have students gather information from the outside world. When we set up relatively large-scale activities with authentic information, these activities are often called *projects*.

Here is an early stage of an extended unit of work for children about space travel:

Space

Make a project on Space.

1 First collect pictures from newspapers, magazines and comics.

2 Make a collage for the cover of the project.

Ex. 8.3 (Hutchinson 1985: 87)

Notice how there is no English language outcome here. In fact, apart from understanding the instruction, this part of the project has nothing to do with English at all! But if the learners are motivated at this point, they will start to search around in their own environment to find pictures of space travel. As they do so, they will remember and discover information which they will bring along to class. This will become available as what we called student material in Chapter 4. As they make their covers for the project, they will be using their creativity to assemble a collage.

> What we hope to get is the depth of personal involvement in meaningful experience which will ease learning.

Projects, above all, are the kind of large-scale activity which teachers can develop in their own situations. What issues concern people where you live?

When it became compulsory to wear seat-belts in cars in Britain, I was teaching a group of European businessmen in England. Some of them were used to wearing seat-belts at home, some were not. Some were in favour of the new law, and some were against. We devised a project to gather together different points of view on the issue. Here are some guidelines you might follow, although not all of them will be relevant for every situation.

- *Make sure that carrying out your project is not going to annoy anyone, either inside or outside your school.*
- *Write down in negotiation with the students a clear statement of the purpose(s) of the project which everyone understands.* Ours were:
  - To gather different points of view on the question: Should seat-belts be compulsory?
  - To make oral presentations of our findings to the rest of the group;
  - To make a written record of our collected findings.
- *Make sure that everyone understands their responsibilities at each stage.* On our project, one group went to the local police station, one group to the hospital, one read newspaper and magazine articles, and one went to a large car park to interview motorists. These sources of information were decided on in discussion in class. In the case of the interviews, the groups agreed to try to make lists of points for and against the compulsory wearing of seat-belts, according to the reasons given. The reading group was particularly interested in finding any evidence that seat-belts really reduced deaths or injuries.

- *Make sure that you have made personal contacts where necessary and that your students will be welcomed where they are going.*
- *Allow lots of time.* Don't get involved in anything but the smallest projects unless you are prepared to give up your own time. Students who get involved in processing real information can become very serious indeed about doing things properly and doing them well.
- *Keep your projected outcomes simple.* This is connected with the last point. We kept our oral presentations and written report to the format:
  - Brief setting of scene;
  - List of opinions plus reasons given.
  The written report was presented to the school for use as possible discussion material with other classes.

There is a particular reason why the memory of this project has stayed with me. At the car park, one group member asked a motorist if she was for or against the wearing of seat-belts. She was strongly in favour. Her son had been killed in a motoring accident.

> We work with reality in order to make things memorable. There are risks involved.

Role-plays and simulations

At its simplest, *role-play* is built into ELT from the earliest stages, when we ask students to say the lines of a dialogue. If we keep this in mind, we can make better use of dialogues by not letting students simply read each line aloud. When students are speaking a dialogue, make sure that they look at the person they are addressing, and that they speak their lines meaningfully.

> Students should speak dialogues, not read dialogues.

As we noted in Chapter 3, we can extend this idea to the saying of items in exercises, too. The functional conversation exercise which we looked at in Chapter 3 (Ex. 3.5), is also a kind of role-play. Notice how, in this example, students are told what they have to do with the language, but not what they have to say.

A further extension of this is when students are given role cards containing information about the person whose part they must act.

For example:

> Work in groups of three. Each person should take one of the roles below.
>
> STUDENT A
> You are a vegan. You strongly disagree with people eating meat, fish, eggs, cheese or milk.
>
> STUDENT B
> You are a vegetarian. You do not eat fish or meat but see nothing wrong in eating dairy products.
>
> STUDENT C
> You are a gourmet. You love good food, including meat, fish and dairy products.
>
> **a)** Work out from the checklist the things you can and can't eat.
> **b)** Compare your diets and try to persuade each other of your point of view.

Ex. 8.4 (Bell and Gower 1991: 108)

Here, we can see how the materials provide an opinion gap in order to produce a situation where communication is necessary. (You can see the work which leads up to this role-play on p. 72.)

But role-play is obviously not simply another information gap activity. The main difference is the element of pretence. What we really hope to gain from role-play is the following:

> Learners can *play-act*. Instead of struggling to say what they mean, they can pretend to mean what they say.

At its best, this means that they can forget about having to take responsibility for the opinions they express. So, allow time to talk through the purpose of role-plays and encourage participants to play at being different characters and to play with the language.

At the same time, we have to allow for the fact that some people will be uncomfortable in this type of activity. With them, explain that this is not a form of theatre: they will not be asked to perform for anyone else. This is a fundamental difference between extended role-play and the speaking of dialogues, where students might well be asked to produce the dialogue with the rest of the class listening.

The other point to make is that a role-play can always be used as a simple practice activity in information exchange if that is the limited investment that students want to make in it.

Like role-plays, *simulations* involve pretence. In simulations, however, students are not so much asked to play at being someone else. They are rather asked to be themselves in an imaginary situation. So, we could say that the roots of simulation lie not so much in given dialogues as in the type of exercise which says:

Look at the following situations and compare your ideas with your partner.

What would you do if . . .
a) someone was following you down a dark street?
b) you saw a pool of blood in your living room?
c) you saw the furniture moving on its own?
d) you heard a noise downstairs at 2 a.m. and you were alone?
e) you were trapped in a lift?
f) you ran out of petrol miles away from anywhere?

Ex. 8.5 (Bell and Gower 1991: 86)

But what we usually mean when we talk about a simulation is an activity in which each participant is given background information, and is then expected to use his or her own skills and values in order to take part. On the next page, for example, is a small-scale simulation in an everyday, social situation.

Ex. 8.6 (Harmer and Surguine 1988: 91)

Simulations are often used on ESP courses to motivate learners by putting them in scenarios which are similar to their work situations.

When setting up a role-play or simulation, the most important things to do are:

- Make sure that everyone understands the purpose of the activity.
- Make sure that everyone understands their own part in the activity. It is often useful in a class where the same role-play will be carried out by a number of groups to begin by getting together

all the players of each role and having them discuss what they understand by the role description and how they intend to act.

- Be available, but not involved unless you are needed to keep the activity going.
- Monitor language use and make notes on student needs.
- Allow time afterwards for people to talk about what happened. This will raise the general awareness of what can happen in role-plays and simulations, and perhaps encourage people to become more involved next time. This sharing is important because it is otherwise often difficult to provide in the ELT class a common experience from which one can expect such widely differing individual experiences.
- Introduce a language focus. This can be based both on student questions and on notes that you have made.
- Allow a lot of time!

Games

What words do you think of when you see the word *game*? I hope that your responses include such words as 'play', 'fun', 'cooperation' and 'competition'. The aims common to all communicative activities, to have people relaxed and enjoying themselves, acquiring language through natural use, as well as making learnt language more readily available, are particularly important here.

When teaching young children, this type of approach is especially relevant, but relaxation and enjoyment are important to all learners, and the most serious of adults can become completely absorbed in cooperating with colleagues in order to win a game.

Here is a simple game involving the use of the Present Progressive to describe current action:

1 Write a list of actions on a piece of paper.

2 Call out one student and show him or her one action on the list (e.g: eating spaghetti).

3 The student mimes the action.

4 Classmates raise their hands if they want to speak.

5 The teacher (the student?) nominates someone, who is allowed one guess, e.g: 'You're opening a bottle.'

6 The student miming responds: 'Yes, I am,' or 'No, I'm not.'

To turn this into a competition, split the class into two halves, one facing the front and one facing the back. A student from each group comes to you for the first word. This student then mimes the action in front of his or her group. As soon as it has been guessed, another student comes for the next word. The game ends when one team gets to the end of your list, or when everyone in the group has had a turn. You appoint an observer to each group to make sure that no one cheats and that the required language is produced on each occasion.

Games are also used for individual, pairwork, or small groupwork. Here, for example, is a word grid game:

Word grid: food and drink

I	C	E	C	R	E	A	M	R	O	P	T	I	K
D	A	Z	O	T	B	P	M	E	A	T	O	D	U
N	K	T	L	R	O	P	I	E	B	E	G	G	S
U	E	A	A	J	E	L	L	Y	Q	A	E	O	A
K	U	L	R	A	R	E	K	C	O	F	F	E	E
B	P	L	U	M	S	S	A	U	S	A	G	E	S

Ex. 8.7 (Rixon 1990: 15)

This is especially useful if you work with learners who are unfamiliar with the roman script, as they start to recognise word shapes in English. An activity such as this can be given to individuals who finish other work early, or made available for self-access use. To encourage cooperation, they can be used for pairwork; if you want to use them competitively, you can set a time limit and see which pair can find the most words in that time.

We have looked at various types of communicative activity: ***tasks, projects, role-plays, simulations*** *and* ***games,*** *which generally involve the gathering, exchange and production of information in English. Such activities are useful because they motivate learners, they further the learning process itself, they provide a context for practice, and they give the teacher information on progress.*

Questions and activities

Think about your responses and then discuss them with a colleague.

1 What experience do you have of communicative activities, either as a learner or teacher? In what ways do these experiences lead you to agree or disagree with points made in the chapter?

2 Can you think of a local project for your teaching situation? You need a question to answer, or a problem to respond to, and different sources of information to draw on. Which students would this be suitable for?

3 Do you find 'play-acting' a useful way to help you relax about what you say, or does it make you even more nervous? Might it be helpful if you had chance to get used to it? Are your feelings common? Are you sure?

4 Look at the role-play and simulation materials. Write step-by-step procedures for using them, similar to the one given for the listening task.

5 What games do you know which could be useful for language learning?

Improving language skills

The communicative activities which we looked at in Chapter 8 involve the use of a broad and integrated range of language skills. While everyone recognises that it is slightly misleading, it remains common in ELT to talk about 'the four skills', by which we mean listening, speaking, reading and writing. You will also find these referred to as *skill areas*, or *macroskills*, each being made up of many *microskills*. We know that people don't learn to use a language by mechanically adding up lots of separate little skills, anymore than they learn by adding up lots of separate structures and functions, but analysing the language into skills gives us more ways of meaningfully focusing our teaching and motivating our learners.

There are two broad ways of viewing the four skills in ELT:

- *The skills are used in learning parts of the language.* For example, when learning a new piece of grammar or a new function, students will listen to the teacher's examples or to a taped dialogue, speak when they perform the dialogue themselves or give their own examples, read the exercises and other source material in their coursebook, and write exercises as a way of helping them learn and remember the new structure. There will also be a communicative activity which involves the learners in integrating the skills, and where the purpose is still to help them practise and learn a certain grammatical or functional usage. And in a less predictable way, we have also seen how students learn the language by being involved in communication, by using the skills which they have.
- *The language is used to help develop the skills.* In this sense, it is possible to concentrate on the teaching in their own right of the skills necessary to:
  - listen to English
  - read English   } and understand what is meant.
  - speak English
  - write English   } and be understood.

This latter perspective is the focus of this chapter.

Listening, speaking, reading and writing are a constant part of people's lives, and we want to use this fact in ELT. We base our skills work, then, around the answers to three questions:

- *What* do people listen to, say, read and write? (Sources)
- *Why* do people do these things? (Motivation)
- *How* do people do these things? (Skills and strategies)

We then work on the question:

- How can we teach these skills and strategies in English?

Before we start working on the answers, it will be helpful to group the skills into two pairs. There are two ways of doing this:

Firstly, listening and speaking can be grouped together, because they are the skills necessary in face-to-face communication. For some learners, this is the main focus of their interest. Reading and writing are the skills necessary in written communication, and this is the main motivation for other learners.

Alternatively, listening and reading can be grouped together, because they are both used to receive language which was produced by someone else. To this extent, we can call them *receptive* skills. In the same sense, speaking and writing are both *productive* skills. As this grouping is based on similarities between the skills themselves, it is the one I shall use in this chapter.

Receptive skills

One of the points in ELT about which everyone agrees is the importance of providing students with large amounts of meaningful language input. As students develop their receptive skills, greater amounts of input become meaningful to them and the greater chance they have of learning the language.

Sources

What do people listen to? One possible list is: advertisements, conversations, descriptions, directions, discussions, drama, films, instructions, interviews, lectures, news, poems, songs, speeches, sports reports, stories, talks, telephone calls and weather forecasts.

What do people read? Apart from some of the items listed under listening, we might add: articles, letters, lists, memos, minutes, novels and reports.

Perhaps you can add more items to these lists. Remember that although some of the items overlap, the language will often be very different. For example, the instructions that you read are expressed differently from the ones that you hear. An important point here is:

> Reading written language out loud is not the same thing as providing authentic listening practice.

Motivation

As a rough generalisation, we can say that people listen and read for two basic reasons: for enjoyment and for information. These are two sources of motivation which we have to work on.

> The more students use their language skills for enjoyment, the more language ability they are likely to acquire.

Listening and reading for enjoyment

What kinds of listening and reading are enjoyable? You have to find this out from your students. What you then have to do is to give them real encouragement to do this kind of listening and reading in English, without building in so many checks and tests that you kill the fun. Here are some ideas which focus on encouraging out-of-class listening and reading, often referred to as *extensive* reading.

- Is there any English language television, radio or cinema in your teaching situation? Agree on a programme or film that you will all see or listen to. Make some class time available to talk about it.
- Is there a continuing serial on radio or television? Go through part of a recorded episode in class and then have a regular spot for keeping up to date with developments.
- If there are subtitled programmes on television, encourage students to experiment with them: sometimes looking at the subtitles, sometimes not, sometimes covering them up.
- Choose a story which you think will appeal to the students and divide it into short (five-minute) episodes. At the end of each class, or as a break in a lesson, read an episode; no questions, no tests.
- Ask friends to record stories in episodes to give the class a change of voice.
- Collect recordings of interesting personal experiences which foreigners have had in the country where you teach. I would advise restricting these to positive experiences.

- Can you provide suitable (= interesting and not too difficult) books?
- Are books available somewhere in the place you teach? Why not? Will the institution buy some? Does it just need some time and a talk with the librarian?
- All the major ELT publishers produce graded readers. Will their local agents help in some way?
- If there is a local British Council Centre or other cultural centre, will they make a special arrangement for your students? What do they do with their old books?
- Will the students (or their families) pay for one book each if you take the trouble to organise the buying of them? If so, talk to a colleague about whether you want to buy a class set (so you can all work together), or a few copies each of a smaller number of books (for groupwork), or as many different books as there are students (to provide maximum variety).
- If you decide for this last option, one way of encouraging participation without overt checking is to ask each reader to mark a card in the book saying how they rate the book on a scale of 1 – 5. Now and again, you can bring together students who have read a particular title and ask them to talk about their reactions.

It is difficult to overestimate the potential effect of having students enjoy English language books or programmes on the radio and television. Unfortunately (or fortunately), however, enjoyment is not something that can be timetabled. What can be timetabled is time for teachers to spend on encouraging the kind of listening and reading that we have talked about here. When students see that the teacher finds something important enough to spend class time on it, they are also likely to take it seriously. If your schedule doesn't allow for this, explain to your director what you would like to do and ask politely if it can be timetabled.

The extra effort required to make language learning a meaningful and enjoyable experience can make all the difference between relative success and relative failure for learners and teacher. It is also one of the factors which make teaching a tiring way to earn a living.

Listening and reading for information

Listening and reading for information is what the usual type of listening and reading class focuses on. Here, we use short texts of spoken or written English in *intensive* listening and reading. As usual, there is a danger to look out for.

Many students have learnt to listen to and read English by working intensively on such passages. The idea of reading which they have formed is one of starting at the first word and battling through till the last, with all elements of comprehension, grammar and vocabulary being tested before the text has been 'done'. If their reading instruction has also featured a lot of reading aloud, this will also have encouraged a word-by-word approach to reading which will, in fact, hold back their progress.

What we want to do is to teach different aspects of reading and listening, sometimes called microskills and strategies. We have to show that we listen and read in different ways, according to our purpose. I read a recipe for a new dish I want to cook very carefully from beginning to end; when I receive my teaching institution's in-house journal, I skim through it very quickly indeed to see if there is anything that I want to spend time on. One strategy is not better than another, they are both appropriate for their purpose.

So, the important question is not:
Did the students learn all the new words in this reading text and answer all the comprehension questions correctly?

The important question is:
Did the students learn skills which will make them better readers of English, or get more practice in the skills of purposeful reading?

> We do not use reading and listening to teach texts, we use texts to teach reading and listening.

As we look at listening and reading in this light, it becomes clear that we need a closer view of the skills and strategies which we wish to teach.

Skills and strategies

The transferable skills we wish to teach will enable students to:

- skim (get a general understanding of what a piece is about);
- extract main points (such as when taking notes on a talk or an article);
- scan for specific information (such as what time the news is on TV);
- comprehend in detail (such as instructions on how to find a house);
- make inferences (about opinions, implications and attitudes);
- evaluate (e.g.: *So what? What have I learnt? What shall I do now?*)

Associated with these skills are many others (recognising the shapes of letters would be one) which I am not going to go into. What we must take account of is the fact that we are dealing with language learners, who may always find themselves in a situation of understanding less than they wish they did. So, we have to encourage an attitude of being confident enough to carry on, even though things remain uncertain. And we need to encourage a strategic approach to dealing with incoming information.

The three major strategies to encourage in students when they are listening and reading for information are:

- Think about your purpose in listening/reading and use appropriate skills.
- Think about what you already know, and keep predicting what the speaker/writer will say next. Keep thinking ahead.
- Focus on what you do understand, and use that to help you work out what you don't understand if it seems important to your purposes.

We have looked so far at possible sources for listening and reading materials, likely purposes for listening and reading, and necessary skills, attitude and strategies. We are now going to look at the shape of a typical lesson in this area, where we bring these various points together in teaching.

The shape of a lesson

The shape of a typical lesson comes from what we know about listening and reading:

- We understand new information in terms of what we already know, think or feel about the subject in question.
- We usually listen and read with some purpose or interest in mind.
- Having new information should involve a change of some kind: we should know more, or think or feel differently from before.

These thoughts suggest the shape of a lesson in three parts:

- *Before text* – We work on the general topic in order to get students thinking about what they already know, and in order to establish a reason for listening/reading.
- *With text* – We use questions and tasks to practise appropriate skills, and to make students aware of those skills.
- *After text* – We ask, 'So what?' In other words, we show some connection between the new information and the students' lives.

Before text

If you have a say in choosing a text, you need to balance topic, difficulty, and task

This is a question of balance, because students can learn a lot from a difficult text if they are motivated by high interest. Also, you can give students a difficult text so long as you only set them a simple task to carry out with that text. Alternatively, you can use a very simple text and set a time limit on what you ask the students to do in order to encourage an increase in reading speed. We shall return to these points when we look at the text itself. One word of warning on the choice of topic:

> Don't assume that what interests you will interest your students. Find out.

Introduce the topic before you move on to the text
When you know which text you will be working with, think of how you will introduce the topic. Pictures are very useful here, or an object that is relevant. Notice how, in the *This is Your Life* materials in Chapter 7, pictures of famous people will be used to introduce a reading task. You might use a written advertisement to introduce a topic when your text is for listening, or a snatch of recorded sound in advance of a reading text.

The purpose is to get students thinking and talking for two reasons:

● As they recall their previous knowledge of a topic, they are preparing themselves to understand new information;
● In these exchanges on the topic, you can elicit or present words that you think will be necessary in dealing with the text.

Establish a purpose for listening or reading
Outside class, we use our language skills for a purpose, and in ELT we always try to establish some kind of purpose when we ask students to use their skills. One way of doing this is to begin with questions or tasks which the students can respond to from their knowledge of the topic, and move on to questions or tasks which demand a knowledge of the text.

Let us look at an example of the points we have made so far. Imagine a text entitled: *The Florida Swamps*. The teacher holds up a picture of an alligator and asks:

1 What's this?
2 Do we have these in our country?
3 Has anyone ever seen one? Where? What was it like? How did you feel?
4 Which (other) countries do they live in?
5 What kind of place do they live in?

6 What other sorts of animal live there?
7 In the United States, where do these animals live?
8 Where exactly?
9 About how many alligators do you think there are in the United States?

Notice how the first three questions draw on the students' personal and national backgrounds, the next three move into general knowledge, and the last three turn towards the text. Some students may know answers to the last questions, some may guess, some may not. The teacher might now say:

10 OK, look at the text and check how many alligators there are in the USA and exactly where they live. I'll give you fifteen seconds.

As well as introducing relevant words, the introductory exchanges have given the reading some context and purpose. The time limit contributes to the development of the particular skill of scanning for specific information. Work on the text has begun.

With text

In another class, the overall topic is the environment, and the class has already carried out this activity:

Work in pairs. Make brief notes on two environmental problems the world is facing at the moment (e.g. *The world is getting warmer.*).

Ex. 9.1 (Bell and Gower 1991: 40)

The students are now told to read a text entitled, 'Are these people criminals?' and are given the following task:

Read the text. Match each of the paragraphs with one of the items in the pictures (e.g. *paragraph 1* refers to *f*). You should be able to work out most of the more difficult words from the context.

Ex. 9.2 (Bell and Gower 1991: 40)

Here is an extract as an example:

Are these people criminals?

1 **F**or a start, Julia Moore's not just killing flies with that spray. By using it, she is helping to create a hole in the ozone layer – the 'gas screen' which helps protect us from the dangerous rays of the sun. The spray is full of chemicals called chlorofluorocarbons (CFCs) that eat up the ozone gas. There are now huge holes in the ozone layer, which is why CFCs should be banned.

2 The cooking pots are boiling over and wasting power. This means that more and more oil and coal has to be burned and this causes pollution and 'acid rain'. 'Acid rain' has already killed more than half of Germany's trees.

3 The vegetables you can see have probably been treated with pesticides – chemicals which kill the small animals and insects that live off them. They have also been fed with fertilisers which can exhaust the soil and kill wild animals. The pesticides and fertilisers end up in our water which is then polluted by them. You can now buy organic fruit and vegetables in many shops which are not treated with chemicals.

Ex. 9.3 (Bell and Gower 1991: 40)

Notice again how the students have been given a simple task to balance the difficult text. This encourages them to keep on reading without worrying too much about the fact that they don't understand all the words. Using this strategy will also help students develop the skill of reading difficult texts for a general understanding or for specific information. As teacher, you could:

- give the students five minutes to do the task individually;
- give them five minutes to check their results in pairs;

- check with the whole class if there are any disagreements (i.e: ask someone for a response, ask if anyone disagrees, ask for reasons before giving any indication whether the response is correct);
- point out how the key items come at the beginning of each paragraph, a common place for important information.

The next activity trains students to develop strategies for working out the meaning of unknown words (see also Chapter 3). Look at the examples in the extracts which you have:

Look back at the text and find these words and phrases which are often associated with the environment. Try to work out their meanings from the context. If necessary, check your answers with a dictionary.

a) *ozone layer* (paragraph 1)
b) *acid rain* (paragraph 2)

Ex. 9.4 (Bell and Gower 1991: 41)

As teacher, you could:

- Do one example with the class, pointing out how the meaning of the word or phrase is actually given, close to it, in the text.
- Tell the students to work in pairs to produce either a definition of each term, or another sentence in which the term is used appropriately. The point of giving the choice is to encourage different kinds of learner to be involved in the activity. (When giving out a task like this, based on a list of items, it is often worth telling different pairs to start the list at a different place: 'You two start with (a), you two with (b), you two with (c), . . . ' etc. This avoids the problem of coming to the feedback stage and discovering that no one has done the last two examples.)
- Ask pairs to give a response which they are pleased with. Try to get a definition and an appropriate usage for each item.

It is important not to go on working with a text until everything has been squeezed out of it. Some students will be reluctant to move on from a text until they feel that they have understood every detail, but a part of learning to read is learning to move away from this dependence on total comprehension.

At the same time, we do not want unhappy students! One possible teaching strategy is to:

- make sure that students are aware of the skills you are teaching;

- explain that your approach means you will read many more texts;
- encourage those who feel a continuing need for total comprehension to use their new skills to work on the texts in their own time.

The exercises we have looked at here are good examples of how modern ELT sets out to teach reading, rather than endlessly test comprehension. If you find that your materials are made up of texts followed by comprehension questions, try to copy some of the techniques you can find in modern ELT books and apply them to your texts. In addition, I suggest a useful way of using test questions for teaching in Chapter 10.

The final task which students are asked to carry out on the above text gets them to practise the skill of extracting the main points:

> List the things which, according to the article, are bad for the environment.

Ex. 9.5 (Bell and Gower 1991: 41)

A procedure of individual or pairwork, followed by a whole-class check, would probably again be appropriate.

The list which the students produce will be, in part, an answer to the question, 'So what?' It will give them a statement of what they now know, having read the text.

After text

The above materials continue in such a way that the students are involved in interviews, discussions and letter writing, using the information which they have gathered from the text.

At this point, however, let us turn to a listening passage for an example of after text activity. Business students have listened to a discussion about recruitment and made notes on five important factors to keep in mind when choosing selection methods. After some intervening work on explicit language study, the students then come to the 'So what?' stage of the lesson, where they are asked to make use of the information they have gained:

> **Transfer**
>
> Design an application form for senior management maximising critical information, but asking only for information that is strictly relevant.

Ex. 9.6 (Brieger and Comfort 1992: 78)

Here, of course, we are clearly concerned with the students' productive skills, and that is where we shall very soon turn.

This section on the receptive skills has focused more on reading than listening. Given the amount of listening practice which learners should be getting from listening to their teacher, along with the greater importance of reading for the majority of English learners in the world, this is probably no bad thing. However, an example of teaching listening is also given in Chapter 8, and a use of a listening text in language practice is covered in Chapter 7.

Finally, it is worth emphasising one obvious difference between listening and reading. With a written text, you can go backwards and forwards at will; it stays there for you. A spoken text is usually only there for the moment it is spoken. If students panic over a few unknown words, they can easily miss the whole point of a message. So, when teaching listening, it is even more important to build up the students' sense of purpose and strategy, coupled with an attitude of confidence in the face of possible uncertainty.

Productive skills

There is disagreement in ELT about the role of speaking and writing. Some people argue that when students produce language, they are showing you what they have already learnt. Some people argue that communicating in the language is a part of the learning process itself. This doesn't have to be a problem. As teachers, we certainly depend on our students' production of language to give us information about their progress. An emphasis on communicative language production will give us this feedback on what they have learnt, while also arguably assisting their learning.

From both perspectives, it is important to use the correction of language as an encouragement and not as punishment. As we discussed in Chapter 7, correction is not a simple matter of comparing student production with standard English and consistently pointing out the differences. Teachers also have to think about:

- which student mistakes are signs of progress for that individual;
- which mistakes a student is ready to learn from;
- whether, when and how to correct.

> Use correction to give students useful information at the right time in the right way to encourage further learning.

Sources and motivation

The types of language which people speak and write are, naturally, the same ones which people listen to and read. Some of them are listed on p. 105, and you may have added more in the meantime. As with the receptive skills, our task is to involve students in the types of language use which motivate them, while teaching them skills and strategies which they will be able to use independently.

Skills and strategies

The most important skills of language production are an ability to:

● develop meanings logically and clearly;
● express unambiguously the function of what you say or write;
● use language appropriate for the people you are addressing.

A necessary strategy for language learners is to develop an ability to:

● communicate ideas which you do not know exactly how to express.
  (See Chapter 3, *Words*, for some suggestions in this area.)

As with the receptive skills, there are also all the microskills of linguistic ability which underlie this level of skill, plus the skills of language learning. Once again, the essential attitude to build is one of confidence in a situation of uncertainty. Let us look at how modern ELT responds to these needs.

Control, freedom and independence

A lot of what we say here will be similar to what we have said in earlier chapters. This isn't surprising, because students have to use language skills to receive the language we are teaching and produce the language they are learning. So, let's try to say some of the same things in a different way.

> The teacher stays in overall control in order to provide meaningful freedom for the learners as they move towards independence.

There are essentially three ways of mixing control and freedom:

● students take a model and personalise it;
● students discuss and plan what they want to say or write;
● students draft, receive comment and redraft.

These ways can be used separately or together. Let us look at some activities which highlight one approach or the other.

Take a model and personalise it

This is also the approach underlying the teaching sequence of Chapter 7. Notice how, in this next example, students are first involved in constructing the model itself, before personalising it.

Copy the text, and put one of these words or expressions into each blank.

after	at midnight	began
finally	as soon as	about
dancing	and then	others
on the night of	some	so
sang	some of them	went

.... December 31st, we invited .... friends to a New Year's Eve party. .... the first guests arrived, we offered them drinks, ... we put on some music. .... half an hour there were .... thirty people in our small flat. .... to dance; .... just went on talking, eating and drinking. .... we all joined hands and .... an old Scottish song called *Auld Lang Syne*; then we went on ....

At seven o'clock in the morning there were still eight people left, ... we had breakfast. .... the last guest went home, and we .... to bed.

Write about a party that you have been to, using at least five of the words and expressions from the box in Exercise 1.

Ex. 9.7 (Swan and Walter 1990: 100)

In this example, the teacher and materials exercise control in order to give the learners a structure inside which they express their own information and imagination.

Discuss and plan

One particularly useful place to practise extended speech is after a piece of groupwork, where all the groups report back to the class. Establishing the report-back stage of the lesson is useful for several reasons:

- the expectation of it concentrates the group members on their task;
- preparation of it encourages the group to reflect on what they have done;
- it ensures that, even if some of the work has been done in a language other than English, the work will be reported in English;
- students take turns to make an extended statement in English.

This last point is the one we want to focus on here. Let us look at the following task:

> **Work in groups of four to try and solve the problem.**
>
> You are a group of eighteen-year-olds. Your parents have agreed to give you holiday money for six weeks if:
> – you all travel together
> – you spend two weeks learning something: for example, a new sport; a new skill (typing, bricklaying, . . .); a foreign language; . . .
> – you camp in the mountains or at the seaside for two weeks.
> Agree on how and where you will spend your six weeks.

Ex. 9.8 (Swan and Walter 1990: 86)

When a group has finished its work, or when the end of the time allowed is approaching, the group can prepare one of its members to make a report. The teacher might want to offer a framework in order to help the report develop clearly. You might say:
Remember to tell us how you are travelling;
where you are going;
how long you are staying;
what you are learning.

The person making the report will be under some pressure while performing in front of teacher and class. The teacher's reaction should be an encouraging one: ignore linguistic mistakes as long as the message is clear. If the message is not clear, rephrase what the student has said and check it with the student, just as you might check what anyone is saying if you are not sure that you understand. So, you might say:
Excuse me a moment, Felipe. Are you saying that you are all learning to ski, or just some of you?

Here, we are reinforcing the suggestion that students can learn from each other. We are using our control to encourage cooperation towards independence.

Draft, comment and redraft
This approach can be used with extended speech, but we shall look at its more common application to written output.

Writing is a more deliberate act than speaking, and it leaves a permanent record, so we want to be careful about how that record looks. On the other hand, we do want learners to make genuine attempts to express themselves in writing even though this will continually lead them to make mistakes. One highly useful approach is to introduce very early the idea of first and second drafts.

So, for this task:

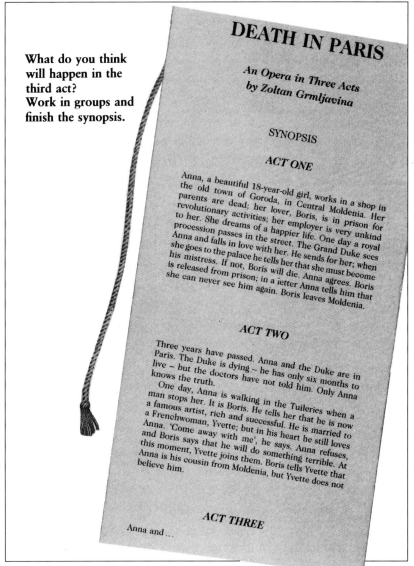

What do you think will happen in the third act?
Work in groups and finish the synopsis.

DEATH IN PARIS

An Opera in Three Acts
by Zoltan Grmljavina

SYNOPSIS

ACT ONE

Anna, a beautiful 18-year-old girl, works in a shop in the old town of Goroda, in Central Moldenia. Her parents are dead; her lover, Boris, is in prison for revolutionary activities; her employer is very unkind to her. She dreams of a happier life. One day a royal procession passes in the street. The Grand Duke sees Anna and falls in love with her. He sends for her; when she goes to the palace he tells her that she must become his mistress. If not, Boris will die. Anna agrees. Boris is released from prison; in a letter Anna tells him that she can never see him again. Boris leaves Moldenia.

ACT TWO

Three years have passed. Anna and the Duke are in Paris. The Duke is dying – he has only six months to live – but the doctors have not told him. Only Anna knows the truth.
One day, Anna is walking in the Tuileries when a man stops her. It is Boris. He tells her that he is now a famous artist, rich and successful. He is married to a Frenchwoman, Yvette; but in his heart he still loves Anna. 'Come away with me', he says. Anna refuses, and Boris says that he will do something terrible. At this moment, Yvette joins them. Boris tells Yvette that Anna is his cousin from Moldenia, but Yvette does not believe him.

ACT THREE

Anna and...

Ex. 9.9 (Swan and Walter 1990: 115)

one procedure would be:

1 Small group discussion of the topic;
2 Feedback of ideas to the whole class;
3 Suggestions for overall organisation of the piece of writing;
4 Students write first drafts;
5 Teacher writes comments/corrections on first drafts;
6 Students work in pairs on revision of first drafts;
7 Students write individual second drafts to submit to teacher for grading, if grades are required.

In this way, the students are encouraged to express themselves, and their writing is taken seriously in that we have shifted the emphasis to include the process of improving what they write. This process is one of the keys to independent language use. The teacher gets feedback on the students' language needs, and the students have a (relatively) standard piece of English as a record.

My earlier comments on correction are particularly relevant again here. Students must realise that you are deliberately drawing their attention to points which you think it will be useful for them to take note of in their second draft. You will not necessarily be turning everything they write into standard English. Your comments on their drafts should include reactions to what the students have to say, not only to how they have said it.

As with the suggestion for reading texts (p. 113), this approach involves a change of thinking as well as of procedure. With reading, I suggested we should not concentrate on each individual text in so great a detail as students might be used to, but should use a greater number of texts for particular purposes to teach generalisable skills. The students' skills are more important than the texts.

Here, I am suggesting that students will produce a smaller number of texts than they might be used to, because each one will go through two drafts. Once again the idea is to teach generalisable skills. This makes demands on the writing tasks themselves – that they should be meaningful and interesting enough for the students to want to express themselves well.

Integrated skills

In theory, we can mix the four skills in any way, but the most common ways for ELT involve some kind of information input, followed by an exchange of information or a discussion, followed by some kind of language output. So the pattern is usually:

> Listen/Read → Converse/Discuss → Speak/Write

This pattern can provide a basis for all kinds of activities in which students can extend their control over the systems of language and the skills of language use. Such activities were discussed in Chapter 8.

I want to close with a few more suggestions regarding the most obvious way in which the skills are integrated, in face-to-face interaction, where listening and speaking interchange constantly. These points relate to the information exchange part of a large-scale communicative activity, and also to straightforward conversation classes that you might find yourself involved in.

Conversations and discussions

You may want to have the whole class together to introduce a topic, and to listen to reports of what was said, but discussion itself takes place most effectively in small groups, where students feel less nervous about speaking and possibly making mistakes.

As far as topics are concerned, a fictionalised topic with a problem often works better than an abstract one. For example, the age at which young people are allowed to marry might be an interesting topic for a group of teenage students, but they might find it difficult to relate to the topic as an abstract issue. If you introduce this topic by telling a story which involves young people who want to marry and parents who want to stop them, and then ask groups to give advice, this is more likely to lead to involvement and communication.

It is often the case that students have things to say, but can't get into a conversation at the right time. You can teach them useful phrases such as, 'I'd like to come in there . . .' by putting such expressions on small cards and giving them out to students. During their discussion, students have to 'play' each card by using the phrase on it in a suitable manner.

A useful extension of this is to have students go through the available cards and choose the ones they would like to try out. If you include phrases such as, 'Let's hear what . . . (*name*) . . . has to say about this' and 'What do you think, . . . (*name*) . . . ?' then students who talk a lot can practise the useful skills of drawing other people into a conversation.

In developing the four skills, we constantly refer to the importance of taking language from relevant sources, and producing language towards relevant ends. These are the keys to motivation. Skills are developed extensively through enjoyment, as well as intensively through accurate study. A lesson on receptive skills will feature work both before and after the actual text being used. A lesson on productive skills will emphasise the processes of production as well as the product itself.

Questions and activities

Think about your responses and then discuss them with a colleague.

1 Think about students with a specific purpose for learning English. Can you make a list of which skills will be most important for them? Check your ideas with a colleague and, if possible, with such a student.

2 Go through the list of ideas for encouraging extensive listening and reading. Choose one. Work out a plan for how you are going to make this happen.

3 Take a reading text and work out some questions which would lead from students' personal experience and knowledge into the text itself.

4 The section *After text* begins by saying that 'students are involved in interviews, discussions and letter writing' using the information from the above text. How might these activities be organised and taught?

5 How does this chapter's comments on control, freedom and independence relate to what Chapter 7 said about careful practice and communication?

6 How many useful conversational expressions can you think of for putting on cards? Can you group them or sequence them in any way for teaching? How would you introduce them?

Testing

Especially at the beginning of their careers, teachers are less likely to be asked to write tests than to use tests and to teach in a situation where test or formal examination results are very important. In this chapter, therefore, we shall look at testing under two headings:

- Using tests;
- Teaching and testing.

Using tests

Purposes

The overall purpose of testing is to provide information about ability and about the learning and teaching process. We can then divide this overall purpose roughly into two:

- *Proficiency testing* – What is this person's level of ability?
- *Achievement testing* – Has this student learnt what he or she is supposed to have learnt according to our teaching?

The main uses of proficiency testing are:

- placement tests – to put new students into the right class;
- diagnostic tests – to find out students' areas of strength and weakness;
- qualifications – when students take a formal examination which exists separate from any course.

The main uses of achievement testing are:

- progress tests – to see how students are getting on in a course;
- end of course tests – to see how well students have learnt what the course set out to teach them;
- course evaluation – to see where the course is more or less successful.

Principles

Probably the most important principle to begin with is one which testing shares with teaching:

There is no single 'best way' of testing, either!

As with teaching, we have to consider the people involved and their backgrounds, as well as the purpose of the test, before we can decide what is appropriate. We then have to take into account certain principles which can help us make decisions in the various contexts in which we work. Testing has terminology which can at first seem quite disheartening, but the terms have developed in order to cover commonsense concepts which we need to understand.

Validity and reliability

A test is valid to the extent that it actually tests what it is supposed to test. So, a valid test of student ability to read and understand English must test exactly and only that ability. If I ask them to write long answers and deduct marks for poor grammar, this reduces the validity of the test as far as reading comprehension is concerned.

A test is reliable to the extent that it produces the same result under the same circumstances. So, if two people of the same ability did the test, or if the same person did it twice, they should score the same.

Subjectivity and standardisation

Validity and reliability usually pull in different directions. Communication is a subjective affair, and tests of communicative ability should include a subjective element if they are to be valid. If I were asked to test two students to discover if they would be able to get by socially on a trip to an English-speaking country, I might decide simply to have a half-hour conversation with them. Such a conversational exchange would be valid, and I would trust my subjective opinion.

But subjective judgements cannot be repeated and repeated consistently, and some tests have to take place on a scale large enough to involve many individual markers. If my colleagues and I had fifty students in the above situation and we had to choose which five would be best able to make the trip, we would need some way of standardising our responses in order to maintain reliability. Although language testing cannot be objective in a real sense, techniques do exist to help standardise marking and the expression *objective testing* is used. (See *Recognition* below.)

As a result of these considerations, we tend to produce tests which balance the elements of validity and reliability, subjectivity and standardisation. And as result of that, as you can see, no test is or can be perfectly valid, or perfectly reliable.

Procedures

It is possible to test people's ability in English by setting a task and seeing whether or not they can carry it out. So, we might say: Students will be able to give accurate directions from Point A to Point B on a street map to someone who cannot see the map.

If a student's directions get you to Point B, the student meets the criterion and passes. This is called *criterion-referenced* testing. It gives you yes/no information about students' specific abilities in English. It doesn't give you detailed linguistic information, nor does it allow you to rank students in a class.

Norm-referenced testing allows us to rank students and it focuses on the language itself in one of two ways:

- by recognition – where you provide language options and ask students to choose the correct one;
- by production – where students have to make up their own language responses.

Recognition

As we have said, recognition items require choice from the students. If there are several options to choose from, this is called *multiple choice* testing. Multiple choice tests are often used for testing discrete points of grammar:

> Please take _ _ _ _ _ _ one of these.
> A: a   B: any   C: the   D: an

A great attraction of testing by recognition is that the marking is quick, easy and, in itself, objective. This means that tests are relatively reliable (in the technical sense we have used above). On the other hand, a lot of people question their validity in terms of exactly what is being tested. Also, good multiple choice questions are very difficult to write.

> Never use your own multiple choice items on students without first trying them out on competent users of English. You will be amazed at the results!

Production

When we ask students to produce language in a test, we often achieve an increase in validity and a loss in reliability. If we return to our fifty students mentioned above, for example, we can say that such an oral interview seems a valid test of their conversational ability, but how can we be sure that it will be reliable?

The short answer is that we can't, and this will remain a difficulty in the testing of language production. However, we have three ways of tackling the problem in order to do the best we can:

Double marking

If we accept that real objectivity is impossible in the testing of communication, our best hope is to get at least two subjective opinions. Where they disagree strongly, we bring in a third. If you are involved in a team which has to test a large number of students in spoken or written English, you should all assess at least a small number of them together.

Analysis

If we break down a piece of writing or speech into different areas of assessment, this might help us make similar assessments of the whole. For the above interview, we might want to think about the separate headings of *pronunciation, grammar, fluency, appropriacy.* Such headings should of course be agreed between colleagues.

Ranking

If we can agree in advance on a scale of ability, we can also use this as the basis for standardising marking. The next step beyond the kind of yes/no criterion which we looked at above is to establish three grades: *unsatisfactory, satisfactory, more than satisfactory.* Many teachers can come to agreement on the basis of these three grades, but circumstances may force you to subdivide each one further. With each further division, we can expect less agreement. To combat this, it can be helpful to agree a description of what you mean by each grade. In terms of pronunciation, for example, you might agree the following typical definitions:

- *More than satisfactory* – No difficulty in understanding what the student said; clear sounds, appropriate stress and intonation.
- *Satisfactory* – Comprehensible, but demands effort from the listener; sounds are sometimes unclear, some sounds pronounced inaccurately, stress and intonation not always helpful.
- *Unsatisfactory* – Frequently couldn't understand what the student said; intonation did not clarify or enliven; monotonous or staccato delivery.

The combined effects of multiple marking, analysis of what is being tested, and agreement on scales of ability can make up in part for the lack of reliability which is inherent in tests of language production.

Cloze tests

Finally, in this section, let us look at one type of test which enables us to pull together several of the points we have made so far, and which can be very useful to teachers who:

- need an idea of the general language ability of a group of students;
- regularly teach the same level of students;
- are involved in placement testing.

The procedure is as follows:

1 Find a text of 400–500 words which you would expect your students to be able to read and understand.
2 Leave the first few sentences intact and then delete every seventh word.
3 Tell students to write in the missing words.
4 Mark each word correct if it is exactly the word originally used by the writer.

You are looking for a text on which the average class score is between 53% and 60%. This indicates that your students should be just about able to read and understand the original text on their own. If you build up a small collection of such texts, you can use them to:

- compare average standards across different groups, and possibly adjust your teaching appropriately;
- check whether new students should join your class, or if they are likely to find the work too easy or difficult;
- help with the future placement of students at the beginning of the next teaching session;
- develop your own appreciation of your students' language abilities as you get better at selecting appropriate texts.

Cloze tests are proficiency tests which are easy to produce, acceptably valid, reasonably reliable and quick to mark. They are also more or less on the borderline between recognition tests and production tests: they certainly call upon the students to produce the missing word, but so much context is given that one could also say that students are called upon to recognise which word is missing. You can go through them and draw out information about discrete points of language use, although their main function is as an integrated test of ability.

We have looked at some important principles and procedures in language testing. We shall now move on to the relationship between teaching and testing.

Teaching and testing

While it is convenient to have a separate chapter about language testing, it is also important to think of testing as a part of the teaching and learning process. A lot of teachers will tell you that testing is the worst part of the job, but that simply confirms that it is part of the job.

Two real problems with testing are that it often involves:

- coming to terms with failure;
- adapting what you do to powers beyond your control.

Coming to terms with failure

Student failure can be just as difficult for teachers as it is for students. To work with people for a year, to get to know them and come to like them, and then to tell them that they have failed an examination which you yourself set and marked: this involves a sort of growing up which non-teachers do not know about.

One distinction which I find helpful to keep in mind is that:

> We teach people and we evaluate language ability. We do not evaluate people.

One lesson to learn is the importance of progress tests. If you are teaching a course which has an examination at the end of it, make sure that you discover as quickly as possible which students are lagging behind and tell them then. If it's too early to use items like the ones they will use in the exam, a cloze test will give you a general indication of ability.

> Be sure to balance warning with encouragement, they are both a sign of your professional seriousness.

Another aspect of poor exam results is that widespread student failure must send you back to look at your course, your teaching and your tests. For many teachers, the only area where they have any influence is their teaching, which brings us to the second problem identified above.

Adapting to powers beyond your control

The effect which tests have on teaching is often referred to as a *backwash* effect. As far as achievement testing is concerned, it is often possible to shape the tests to the teaching or, even better, to shape the teaching and the testing together in the most appropriate way for the students taking a course. Placement testing and diagnostic testing occur before teaching, when backwash is not such a direct issue. It is with formal examinations however that backwash becomes important, and where backwash can become a problem.

When you teach an exam course, you take on an extra responsibility. The students in your class have a right to expect you to help them pass that examination. There are two extreme positions here, both of which are honourable. The first one expresses a sense of responsibility to the principles of good teaching, and says:
I teach them English the best way I can, and with that English they ought to be able to pass any exam.

The second expresses a sense of responsibility to the students and says:
The students are here to pass the exam, so that is what I teach them. They can worry about 'communicative ability' when they need it.

The first position runs the risk of sacrificing the students to educational principles. The second runs the risk of teaching an examination and perhaps killing off any further interest in the language.

Because it involves personal loyalty to students, and because exam failure by students is also very threatening to teachers, the second position is more common. This is why, if teaching and testing are in conflict, testing is more powerful. ELT is full of teachers trying to teach well in the context of tests which pressure them to teach badly.

Let's look at some ways in which we might find a useful way forward.

- *Talk to the students about the situation* – Remember that you may know what is going on in class and how it relates to an examination, but the students might not. And that situation is repeated with every new class.
- *Be positive* – As with materials, you can work with your colleagues to change a bad exam, but don't be negative about it with the students.

- *Get to know the examination* – You should certainly make yourself and your students familiar with old examination papers, but also find out if there is a written statement somewhere of what the exam sets out to test.
- *Distinguish between language skills and examination techniques* – Let us think about an examination which is made up mostly of multiple choice grammar items. Students might worry about spending time on communicative activities. You can point out that the activity is for language learning, and that you will cover the necessary exam techniques in your language focus after the activity.
- *Use exam techniques as the basis of communicative activities.*
  - Any recognition item which requires choice can be a basis for discussion in pairs or groups, or all together.
  - Any test item which requires the production of language is the basis for cooperative preparation and redrafting in pairs or groups, or all together.

What is more, by relating discussion and cooperation to examination techniques, you can help to take away the mystery and the threat from examinations. Here is one technique for working on multiple choice grammar tests:

1 Collect common mistakes as you listen to group activity.
  e.g: *I live here since January.*
2 Write each sentence on the board/OHP with a blank where the mistake was.
3 Elicit suggestions for filling the blank and write them all on the board.
4 Ask for typical mistakes and write them on the board.
5 Have students talk about and choose one or more possible answers.

This technique is useful for raising grammatical awareness and demystifying multiple choice questions. It can also make students more aware of the importance of context as they see different possibilities fit into the frame.

Some of the main problems with language testing probably arise from the fact that so many teachers dislike testing so much that they leave it in the hands of people who don't have much interest in teaching.

> If you work in a situation where you believe that change is needed in ELT and you want to work for that change, get involved in testing.

A change in an examination can have a bigger effect on teaching than any number of books about methods. But remember, too, that a responsible attitude to change demands a lot of support for teachers who have been teaching to the old exam for their own good reasons. And that leaves us with another reason for not basing our teaching too solidly on examinations: they do change eventually.

'Testing', like 'correction', is a word with negative overtones for many people. The two challenges we face are, firstly, to make testing an acceptable way of gathering useful information which can help learners and teachers alike and, secondly, not to let formal examinations get in the way of good teaching.

Questions and activities

1 Look at some test items and ask yourself exactly what is being tested. To what extent does the test seem valid to you? What attempts have been made to standardise the marking?

2 Write some multiple choice items of your own to test knowledge of vocabulary, knowledge of grammar, and reading comprehension. Try them out with colleagues or friends and find out if they agree or disagree with all your choices.

3 Make up a cloze test for a class that you teach. Check the results against your intuitions regarding overall ability.

4 Have you ever failed an examination? What did you think about the teacher's role in your failure?

5 *I . . . here since January. (to live)*: Which verb forms are possible?

Development

For some people, ELT is an occupation for a few years. I hope that this book will be useful to them. But for a great many teachers, ELT is what they do throughout their working lives. As in any job, routine and repetition can lead in time to feelings of boredom and pointlessness. If this book is to succeed as an introduction to ELT in these terms, it must encourage readers to get involved in a process of continuing personal and professional development.

In this section, I discuss some points which are important to such development: reading, cooperation, investigation and qualifications.

Reading

A good way of supporting your development as a teacher is to read an ELT magazine or journal on a regular basis. Some well-known ones from Britain are: *Practical English Teaching* and *Modern English Teacher*, both of which are mostly concerned with suggesting classroom procedures, and *ELT Journal*, which has longer articles with more space for discussion.

From the USA, *Forum* has a mixture of classroom tips and discussion articles, while *TESOL Quarterly* presents much longer and usually more academic pieces.

All of these journals contain review sections, which can help you decide which books you might want to buy. There may also be a local teachers' journal in your area.

Cooperation

The most effective means of development for a teacher involve some kind of cooperation with other teachers. The most effective form of cooperation involves attending each other's classes: an emotive issue which we raised in Chapter 1.

This would be one way of beginning:

1 Invite a friend to visit one of your classes. Choose a class that contains something you enjoy doing, or something new that you want to try out, or something that you find difficult. Explain to your friend what you are going to do and ask him or her to concentrate especially on this part of the lesson.
2 After the lesson, explain to your friend what you think went well or badly, what you learnt from it, and what you intend to do next. Perhaps you want to try the same thing in a different way. Perhaps everything went so well that you now want to concentrate on another part of your teaching.

By sharing your experience and giving you the chance to reflect on it and clarify the next step, your friend has already helped enormously. If you want a more direct contribution, you can ask your friend:
'Is there anything that you do with your students that you think would be relevant to what I am trying to do here?'

Notice that the visitor is still not being asked to evaluate what the teacher has done. That responsibility remains with the teacher him or herself. Of course, if you want criticism, praise, advice and suggestions from your visitor, that is up to the two of you to work out.

> The important point is to put an end to the isolation of teachers in their classrooms and to begin open cooperation.

To take a broader view of cooperation, an important step towards continuing development is to join a teachers' association. The two main international ELT associations are the British-based *International Association of Teachers of English as a Foreign Language (IATEFL)*, and the USA-based *Teachers of English to Speakers of Other Languages (TESOL)*, whose addresses are at the end of this chapter. There will probably be a national association for you to join, and perhaps a more local teachers' group. The last of these is the most important for you to support, because this is where realistic responses to significant local issues can develop.

Investigation

You can extend your cooperation with a colleague into a more serious investigation of your teaching. This would be a way to begin:

Keep notes on all the following stages.

1 Choose an area of your teaching that particularly interests you (e.g: reading comprehension).
2 Focus on one small part of this work (e.g: dealing with new vocabulary).
3 Make a study of what you do at the moment (e.g: invite a colleague to watch you, make a recording and explain to a colleague what was going on, or ask your students what they most and least value about this part of your teaching).
4 Gather ideas about this area of teaching (e.g: talk to colleagues, read).
5 Plan something different to what you usually do and try it out in class, preferably with a colleague there, or with a recording.
6 Think about what happened and check your impressions with a colleague and/or with your students. Try to express what you have learnt in writing if possible.
7 Decide whether to continue focusing on this area of your teaching or to move to another.
8 Compare your notes with other colleagues who are interested in classroom innovation and their own development.

Note the links between investigation, cooperation and reading, as they all contribute to teacher development. Notice, too, the ways in which this procedure brings together knowledge from books, knowledge from experience, and knowledge from other people, while asking you to take responsibility for answering the question, 'What can I learn from all this?'

We also have to remember to respect the different attitudes and opinions which we will meet. You may want to make major changes in your teaching situation. If you do, remember that change is very slow, especially if other people are not convinced of the need for change. And there is no benefit in using methods of teaching which are so unfamiliar to the learners that they cannot accept and trust you as a teacher. So, to some extent, you may have to change yourself to suit your situation. If you do, remember that you will be at your best when what you are doing is in tune with what you believe in.

> The best approach is one which inspires teacher and learners with confidence. As teacher, you have to take most responsibility for finding that way again and again.

Qualifications

ELT is offered in many countries as either the major or subsidiary topic of a formal teaching qualification. People who train in this way have the advantage of seeing their specialisation in its fuller educational context. Outside the field of formal, full-time education, there is also now a reasonably well-developed track of qualifications in the British system, which has gained a degree of international recognition. At its most basic, the components are:

A certificate

An introductory qualification of at least 100 hours of tuition, often taken in an intensive four-week block. This is mostly for candidates with no teaching experience, and is seen as an initial qualification, after which graduates should be given on-the-job support. One might describe this as an 'apprenticeship' level. Some teachers of other subjects use this qualification as a way of shifting into ELT.

A diploma

These courses are usually of about the same length as the Certificate courses when taught in an intensive block, but they are also often taught part-time over an academic year. They are aimed at experienced ELT teachers, usually graduates, who want to formalise and gain recognition of their expertise as independent professionals.

Whatever teaching qualification you study for, make sure that you understand how you will be assessed, but do not let that dominate your thinking: give your teachers a chance to help you learn. Having said that, let me conclude this section with some advice on the two probable forms your assessment will take.

There should certainly be a *practical assessment*, where someone watches you teach. You should make every effort to:

- know your students;
- know the assessment form your examiner is using;
- talk to the examiner before the class about what you are trying to do, and after the class about how you think it went.

This last point is very important. Things can go wrong in anyone's class. An examiner will be impressed by a teacher who shows an awareness of what went well and what did not.

As far as the assessment form is concerned, you should try to discuss it with your colleagues and your teachers, and try it out on your colleagues' classes and on videoed classes if possible. The important part of this is the discussion afterwards, as you try to move towards an agreed idea of what good teaching is like.

Formal writing will also probably be a part of your assessment. Examiners will want to see a response to two questions:

- *How* do you act in a certain area of ELT?
- *Why* do you think that that's a good idea?

Firstly, if you are writing to a given title, do make sure that you read it carefully. In all probability, the title will suggest not only the required content of your answer, but also how you might organise it. Let us look at a possible example:

> What are the advantages and drawbacks of groupwork?
> Describe two techniques involving groups which you find useful with your students.

This suggests a section on 'advantages' which will explain the principles behind the desirability of groupwork. The section on 'drawbacks' will show an awareness of the difficulties involved in implementing these ideas. The 'two techniques' will involve different areas of language teaching and types of groupwork in order to show the breadth of your expertise. The descriptions will show how you gain some of the benefits of groupwork while overcoming as best you can the difficulties of implementation.

If you have time, you add an introductory paragraph which tells the reader exactly how your response is organised and a final paragraph which reminds the reader of the main points you have made.

Simply by following the wording of the question, you have a highly-organised response to delight the heart of the most overworked examiner. If this seems insultingly simple, I can only tell you that it is all too rarely done.

Next, if you are free to choose your own topic for an assignment, choose a small one! Even if you are worried about how you can possibly produce as many words as the assignment demands, that is unlikely to be your problem once you start writing. I have never known anyone have a problem with a topic because it was too small. If you choose a topic such as 'Teaching Writing', you will have no space in which to say anything interesting at all; you will find yourself simply repeating superficial generalisations.

If you choose a topic such as 'A peer-correction technique for an intermediate writing class', you should have the space to write about what you do and discuss other possibilities that you know about. This should help you keep a focus on the principles and procedures of actual teaching, which is what your examiner will want to see.

Organisation remains very important. Try thinking about what you want to say in these terms (adapted from Hoey 1983):

- *Situation*
  Setting – where you work, type and level of students, etc.;
  and/or
  State – what usually happens in a certain area of ELT;

- *Focus*
  Problem – something unsatisfactory about the Situation, or some difficulty that you face or faced;
  and/or
  Purpose – an aim or objective that arises or arose for you;

- *Response*
  Procedure – what you did, or what you intend to do about the Problem or Purpose;
  and
  Principle – your reasons and arguments for the Procedures;

- *Evaluation*
  Evidence – what data can you produce to show that your Response was a good one?
  or
  Criteria – if you are writing about the future, how will you go about evaluating your Response?

This is, of course, only one way of organising a piece of writing. It is, however, a very powerful one, and useful both for reader and writer.

---

*This chapter has focused on your continuing development as a teacher. The general suggestion is that you cooperate with others to explore your own teaching situation, make your own discoveries, and take responsibility for acting on them. You can support this process by your reading and, if you wish, by formal study. There are strong links between what we are saying here about teachers and what we said about learners and strategies in Chapters 1 and 2. Learners and teachers are united again by the importance in their lives of **awareness, self-development** and **empowerment**. As ever, such strands of development as I* *have highlighted need to be rewoven in order to be experienced at their strongest.*

Useful addresses

The teachers' associations mentioned in Chapter 11 are:

IATEFL
3, Kingsdown Chambers,
Kingsdown Park,
Tankerton CT5 2DJ.
England.

TESOL
Suite 205,
1118 22nd Street NW,
Washington DC 20057.
USA.

For more information about teaching certificates and diplomas, contact:

University of Cambridge Local Examinations Syndicate (TEFL Dept.)
Syndicate Buildings,
1, Hills Road,
Cambridge CB1 2EU.
England.

Trinity College London
16, Park Crescent,
London W1N 4AH.
England.

Questions and activities

This chapter is full of suggestions for teacher activity. The only real question is, 'What are *you* going to *do*?'

Further reading

If you want a general book which treats the field of ELT at greater length and in greater depth than this introduction can, I strongly recommend Harmer (1991), an excellent handbook for the skilled teacher. Here are some other recommendations which you could use to follow up particular interests which arise from the different chapters.

Chapter 1
Stevick (1989) is a book of interviews with successful language learners, along with commentaries on their different ways of learning. Wright (1987) provides ideas and activities which relate the roles of learners and teachers.

Chapter 2
Stevick (1980, 1982, 1986) is always good at weaving together the different strands of ELT into sensible and sensitive ideas for teaching. Ellis and Sinclair (1989) provides useful materials for explicit learner-training.

Chapter 3
Morgan and Rinvolucri (1986) is a good teacher's resource book for the teaching of vocabulary. Alexander (1988) is a reliable and traditionally organised reference grammar. Swan (1983) takes an alphabetic, problem-solving approach. Harmer (1987) is dedicated to the teaching of grammar, and Frank and Rinvolucri (1991) is a good teacher's resource book on the same subject. Swan and Smith (1987) describes problems which speakers of various languages have when learning English. Kenworthy (1987) will be useful if you become particularly interested in pronunciation, while Cook (1989) relates discourse analysis to ELT.

Chapter 4
Grant (1987) is excellent on how to use and supplement the textbook, and Wright and Haleem (1991) gives clear and sound advice on how to produce attractive classroom materials.

Chapter 5
Underwood (1987) and Wright and Haleem (1991) both have more to say on most of the issues of environment and equipment raised here.

Chapter 6
Underwood (1987) deals with classroom management and Byrne (1987) investigates interaction in much more depth and with lots of ELT techniques. Nolasco and Arthur (1988) covers ELT in general from the perspective of large classes, where good management is particularly important. Davis and Rinvolucri (1990) offers ideas for negotiating social rules with students.

Chapter 7
Read articles in the journals referred to in Chapter 11 and see how they relate to Chapter 7's overall methodological approach. Larsen-Freeman (1986) gives an overview of different specific methods of ELT. Edge (1989) gives more ways of correcting spoken and written English in line with the ideas here.

Chapter 8
Scott and Ytreberg (1990) is good on the use of activity in the teaching of children, where it is especially important. You can get lots of ideas for project work from Fried-Booth (1986) and for role-play from Ladousse (1987). For advanced learners, Hadfield (1987) offers a wide range of communicative games which involve elements of all the activities discussed here.

Chapter 9
Anderson and Lynch (1988) investigates listening, and Bygate (1987) speaking. Holme (1991) and Hess (1991) are collections of ideas for involving students in their reading texts. Byrne (1986, 1988) are well-established books on teaching oral and writing skills. White and Arndt (1991) is good on the whole process of writing, from generating ideas to redrafting. Ur (1981) has proved useful in the area of conversation and discussion.

Chapter 10
Heaton (1990) is a clear and straightforward guide to the writing and use of language tests.

Chapter 11
IATEFL has a Teacher Development Special Interest Group which produces its own newsletter, and Allwright (1988) will be useful for teachers who want to form a local association. Brumby and Wada (1990) investigates team-teaching in Japan and gives advice which has a much broader application. Edge (1992) is a book of ideas and materials designed to further professional cooperation and development in ELT.

The most profound yet practical body of work on ELT is that of Earl Stevick. The first two chapters of Stevick (1980) would be a good place to start and, with great respect and thanks, that is where I should like to finish.

References

Abbs, B and Freebairn, I 1990 *Blueprint*, Longman.
Alexander, L G 1988 *Longman English Grammar*, Longman.
Allwright, R (ed.) 1988 *Developing an Association for Language Teachers: An Introductory Handbook*, University of Lancaster.
Anderson, A and Lynch, T 1988 *Listening*, OUP.
Bell, J and Gower, R 1991 *Intermediate Matters*, Longman.
Brieger, N and Comfort, J 1992 *Personnel*, Prentice-Hall International.
Briggs-Myers, I 1980 *Gifts Differing*, Consulting Psychologists Press.
Brumby, S and Wada, M 1990 *Team Teaching*, Longman.
Bygate, M 1987 *Speaking*, OUP.
Byrne, D 1986 (2nd. ed.) *Teaching Oral English*, Longman.
Byrne, D 1987 *Techniques for Classroom Interaction*, Longman.
Byrne, D 1988 (2nd. ed.) *Teaching Writing Skills*, Longman.
Cook, G 1989 *Discourse*, OUP.
Davis, P and Rinvolucri, M 1990 *The Confidence Book*, Longman.
Edge, J 1989 *Mistakes and Correction*, Longman.
Edge, J 1992 *Cooperative Development*, Longman.
Ellis, G and Sinclair, B 1989 *Learning to Learn English*, CUP.
Frank, C and Rinvolucri, M 1991 *Grammar in Action Again*, Pilgrims/Prentice Hall.
Fried-Booth, D 1986 *Project Work*, OUP.
Grant, N 1987 *Making the most of your Textbook*, Longman.
Hadfield, J 1987 *Advanced Communication Games*, Nelson.
Harmer, J 1987 *Teaching and Learning Grammar*, Longman.
Harmer, J 1988 *Meridian Plus 1*, Longman.
Harmer, J 1991 (2nd. ed.) *The Practice of English Language Teaching*, Longman.
Harmer, J and Surguine, H 1988 *Coast to Coast 3*, Longman.
Heaton, J B 1990 *Classroom Testing*, Longman.
Hess, N 1991 *Headstarts*, Longman.
Hoey, M 1983 *On the Surface of Discourse*, Unwin.
Holme, R 1991 *Talking Texts*, Longman.
Hutchinson, T 1985 *Project English*, OUP.
Kenworthy, J 1987 *Teaching English Prononciation*, Longman.

Ladousse, G 1987 *Role Play*, OUP.

Larsen-Freeman, D 1986 *Techniques and Principles in Language Teaching*, OUP.

Longman Active Study Dictionary of English 1991 Longman.

Mohamed, S and Acklam, R 1992 *Beginners' Choice*, Longman.

Morgan, J and Rinvolucri, M 1986 *Vocabulary*, OUP.

Nolasco, R and Arthur, L 1988 *Large Classes*, Macmillan.

Rixon, S 1990 'Puzzle it out', *JET* 1.1, 15f.

Scott, W and Ytreberg, L 1990 *Teaching English to Children*, Longman.

Stevick, E W 1980 *Teaching Languages: A Way and Ways*, Newbury House.

Stevick, E W 1982 *Teaching and Learning Languages*, CUP.

Stevick, E W 1986 *Images and Options in the Language Classroom*, CUP.

Stevick, E W 1989 *Success with Foreign Languages*, Prentice-Hall International.

Swan, M 1983 *Practical English Usage*, OUP.

Swan, M and Smith, B (eds.) 1987 *Learner English: A Teacher's Guide to Interference and Other Problems*, CUP.

Swan, M and Walter, C 1990 *The New Cambridge English Course 1*, CUP.

Underwood, M 1987 *Effective Class Management*, Longman.

Ur, P 1981 *Discussions that Work*, CUP.

Watcyn-Jones, P 1981 *Pair Work, Student A and Student B*, Penguin.

Wenden, A and Rubin, J 1987 *Learner Strategies in Language Learning*, Prentice-Hall International.

White, R and Arndt, V 1991 *Process Writing*, Longman.

Wright, A and Haleem, S 1991 *Visuals for the Language Classroom*, Longman.

Wright, T 1987 *Roles of Teachers and Learners*, OUP.